Mandala Inspired Coloring Book

by Jonathan Wilkins

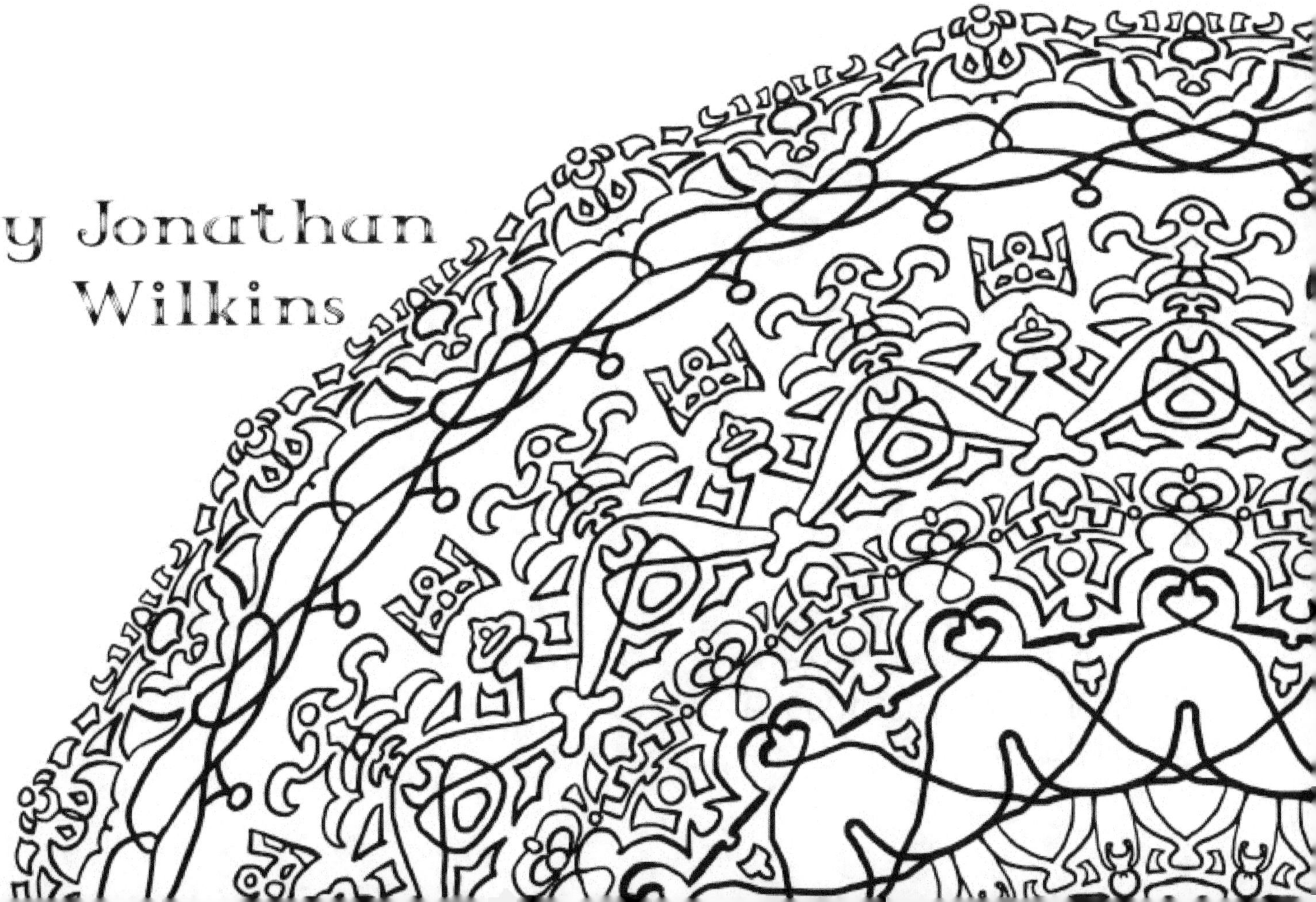

This book is dedicated to colorers everywhere

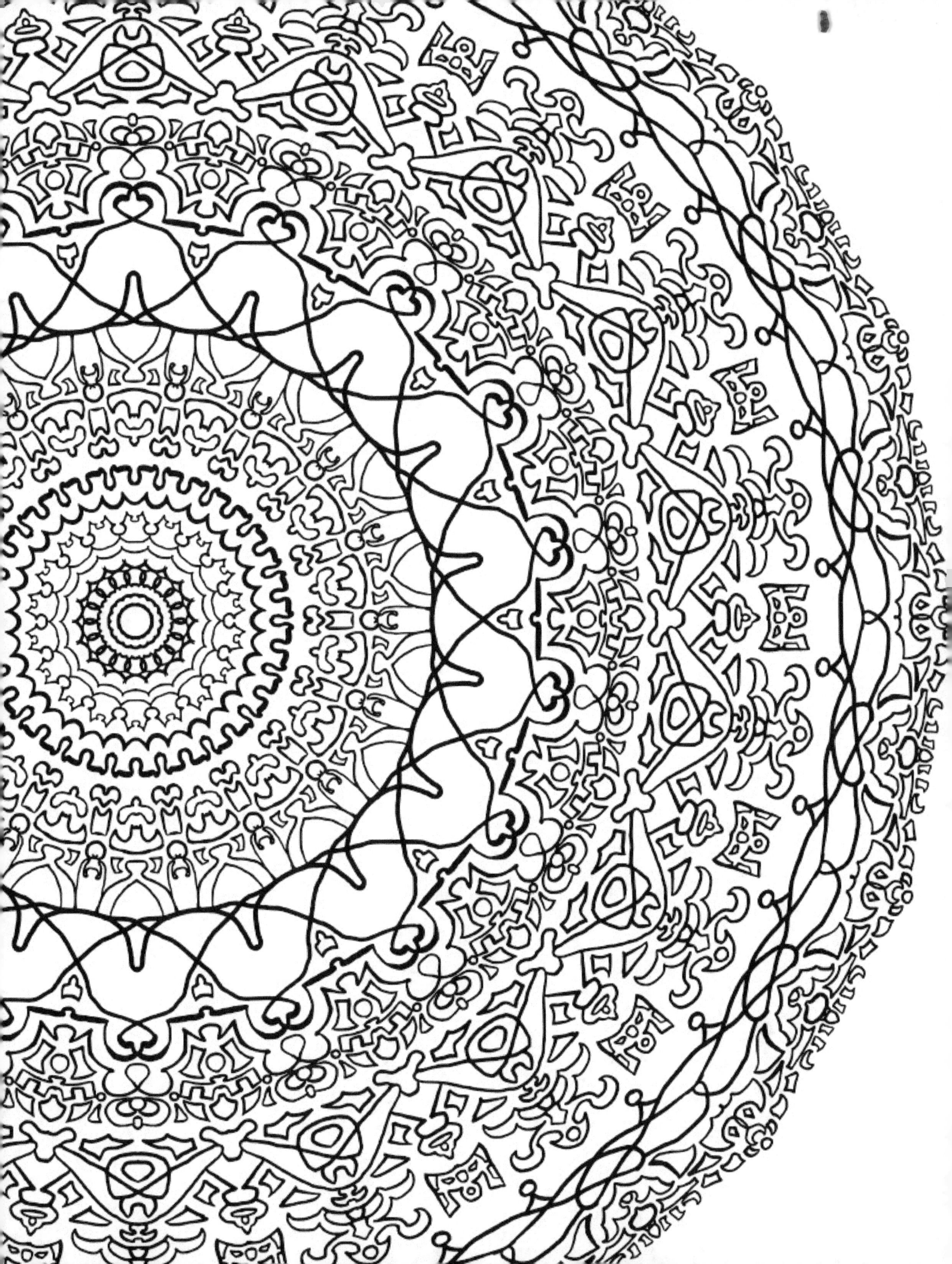

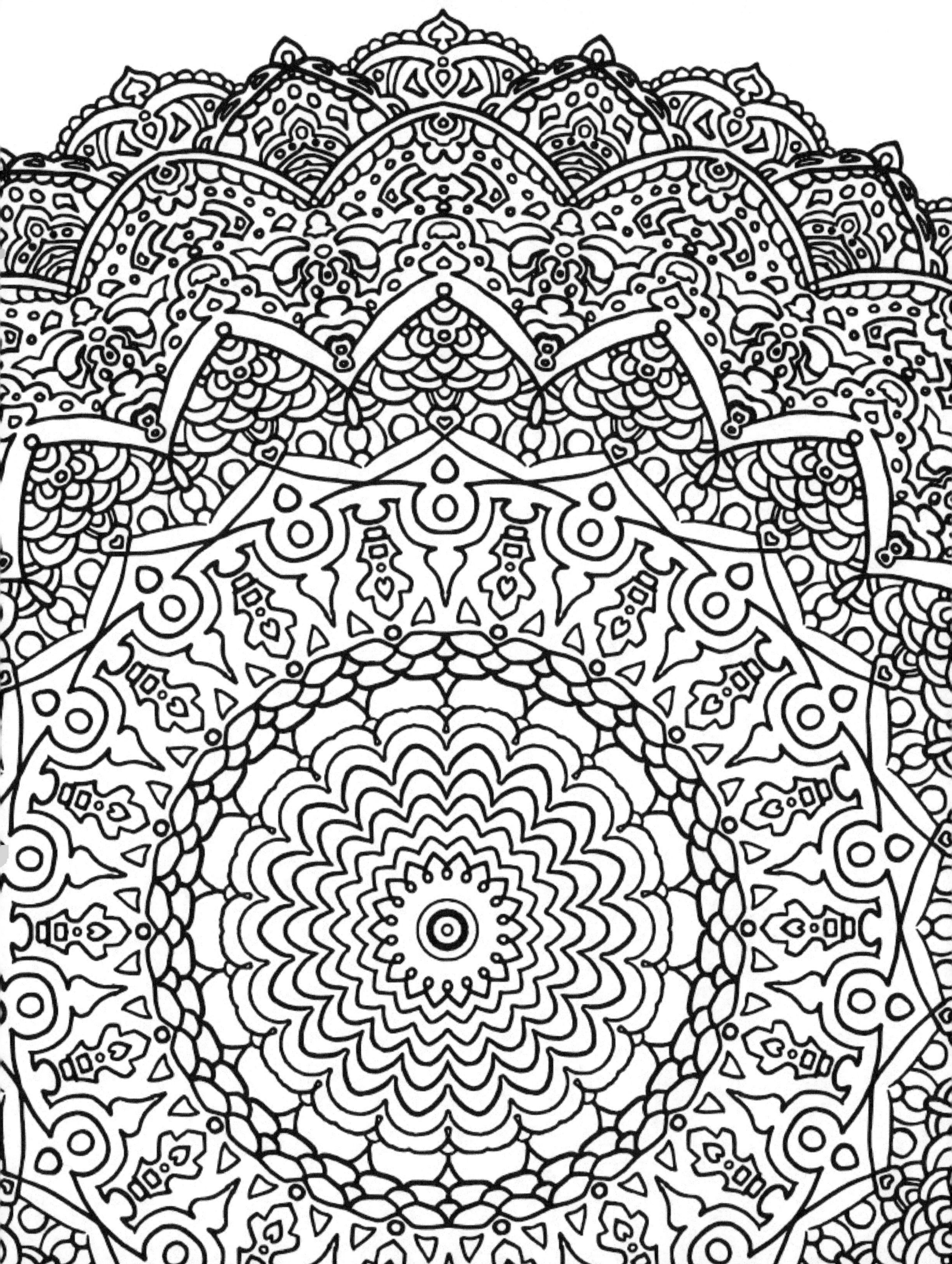

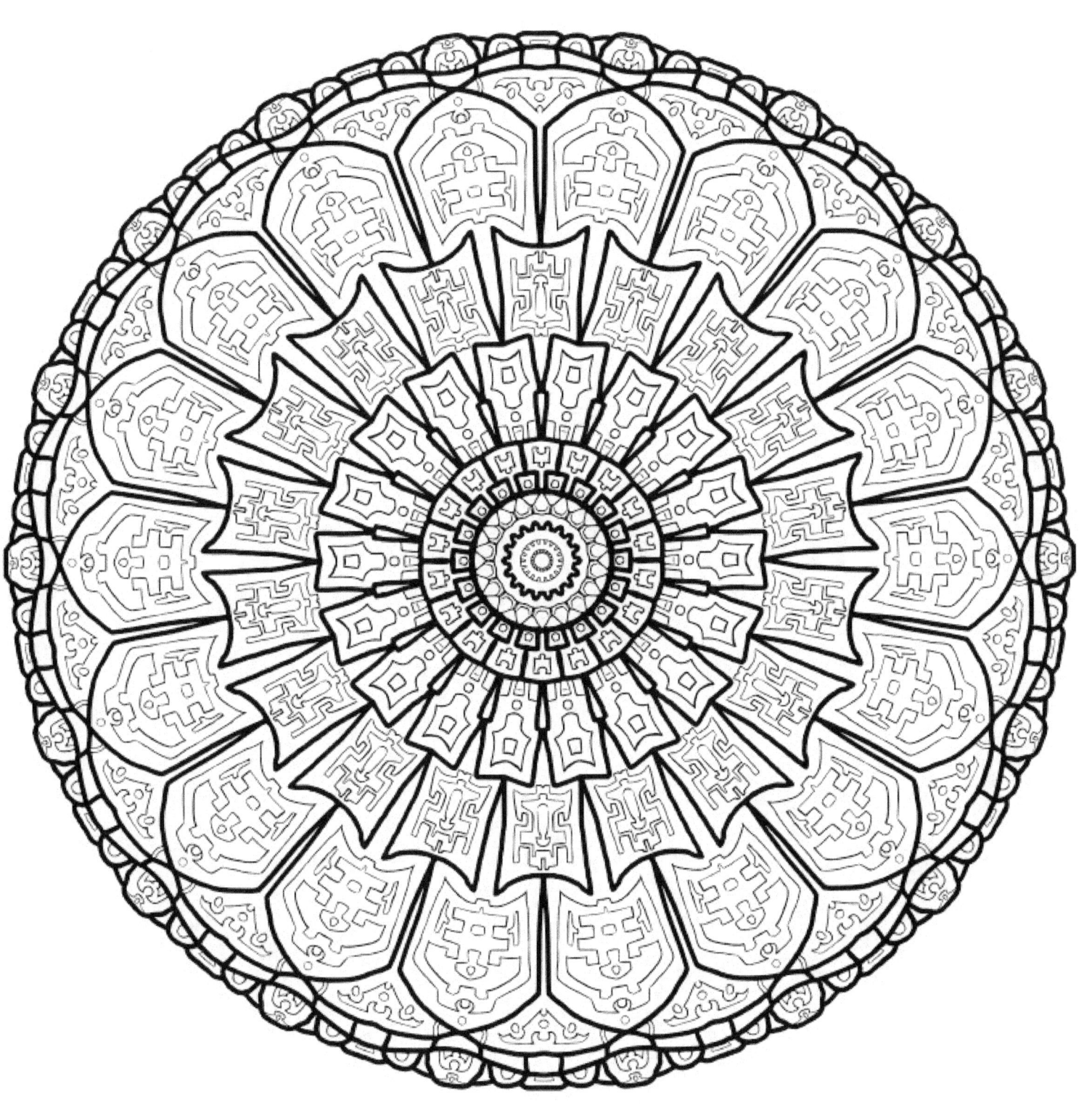

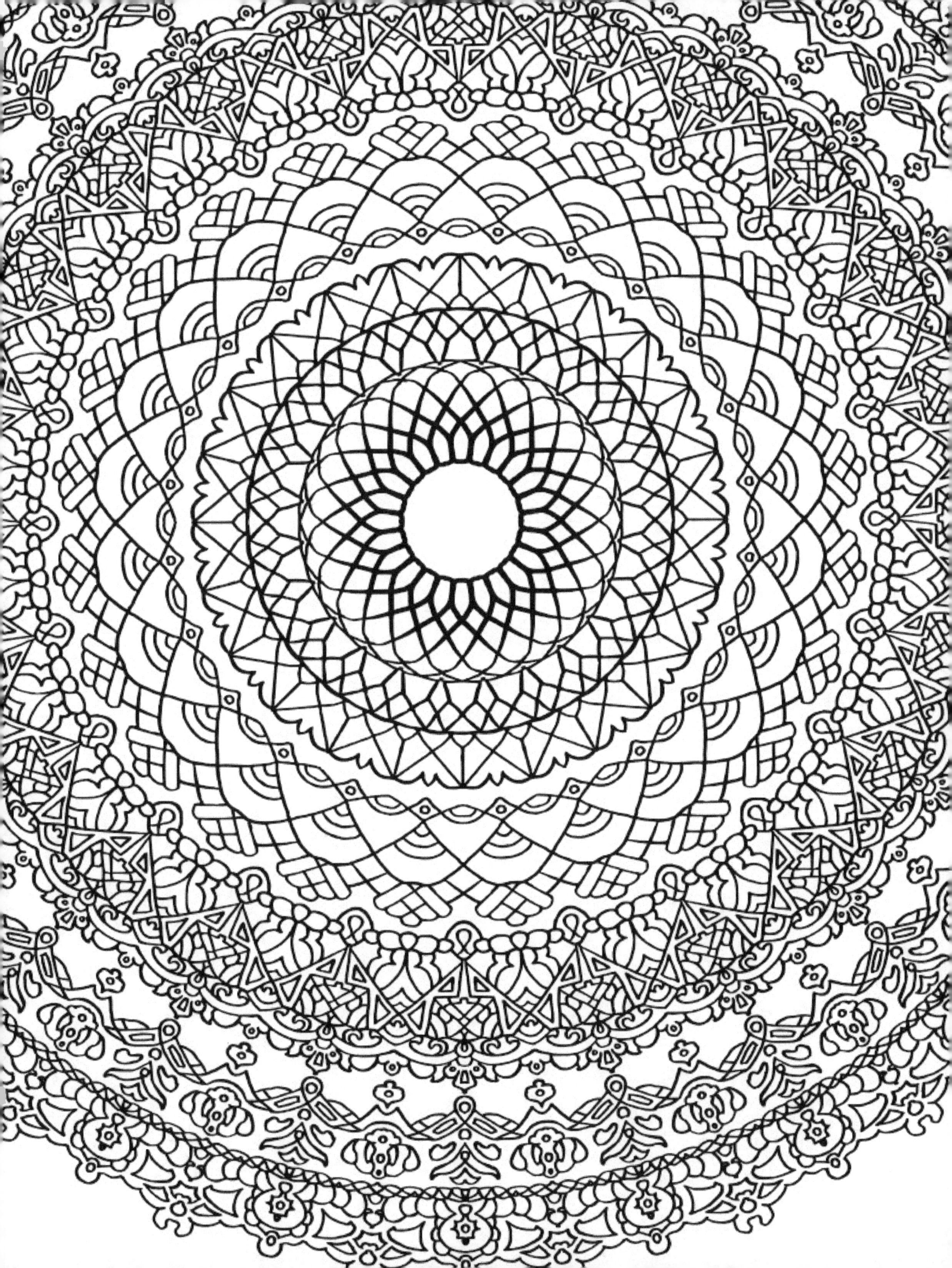

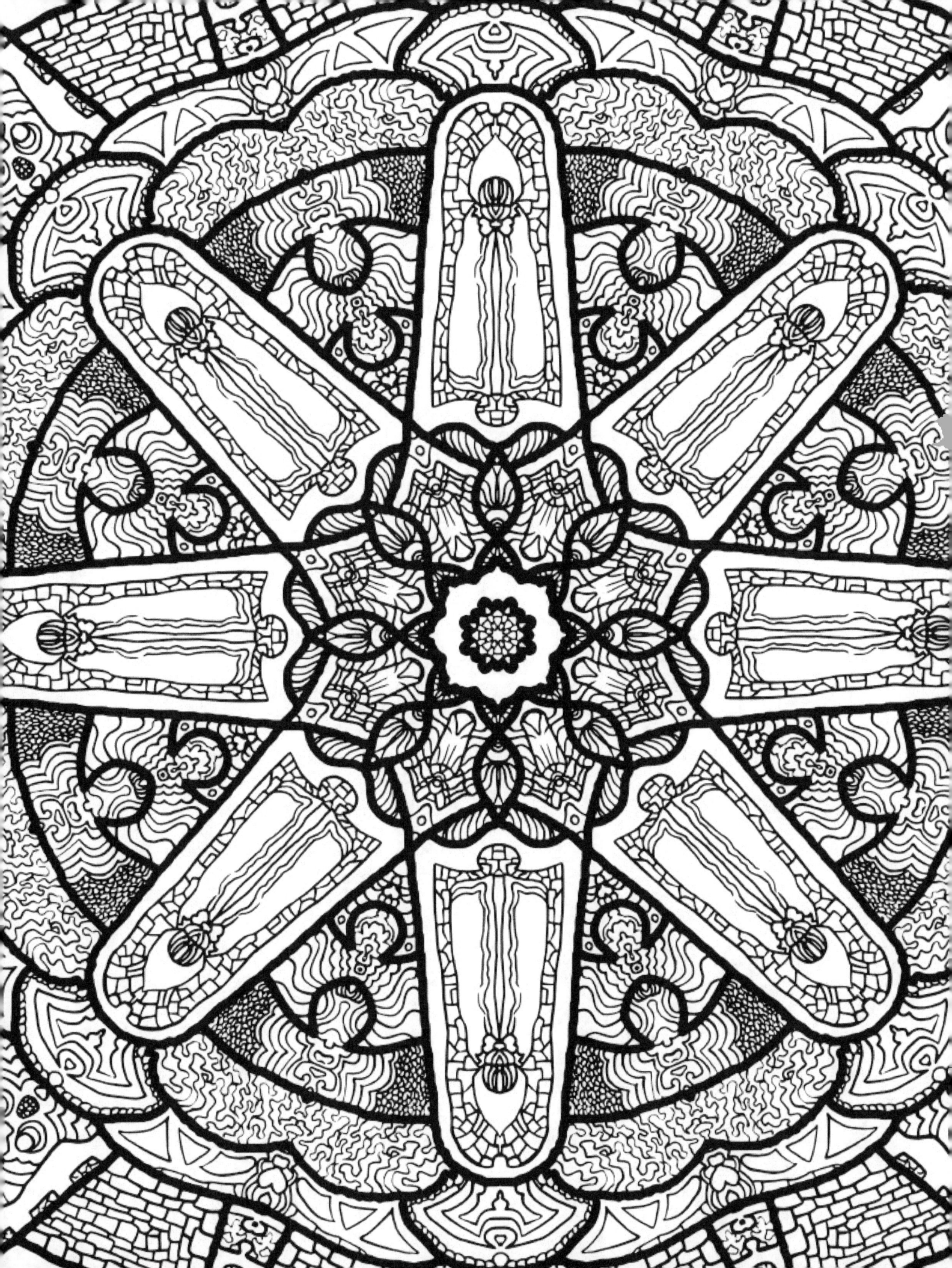

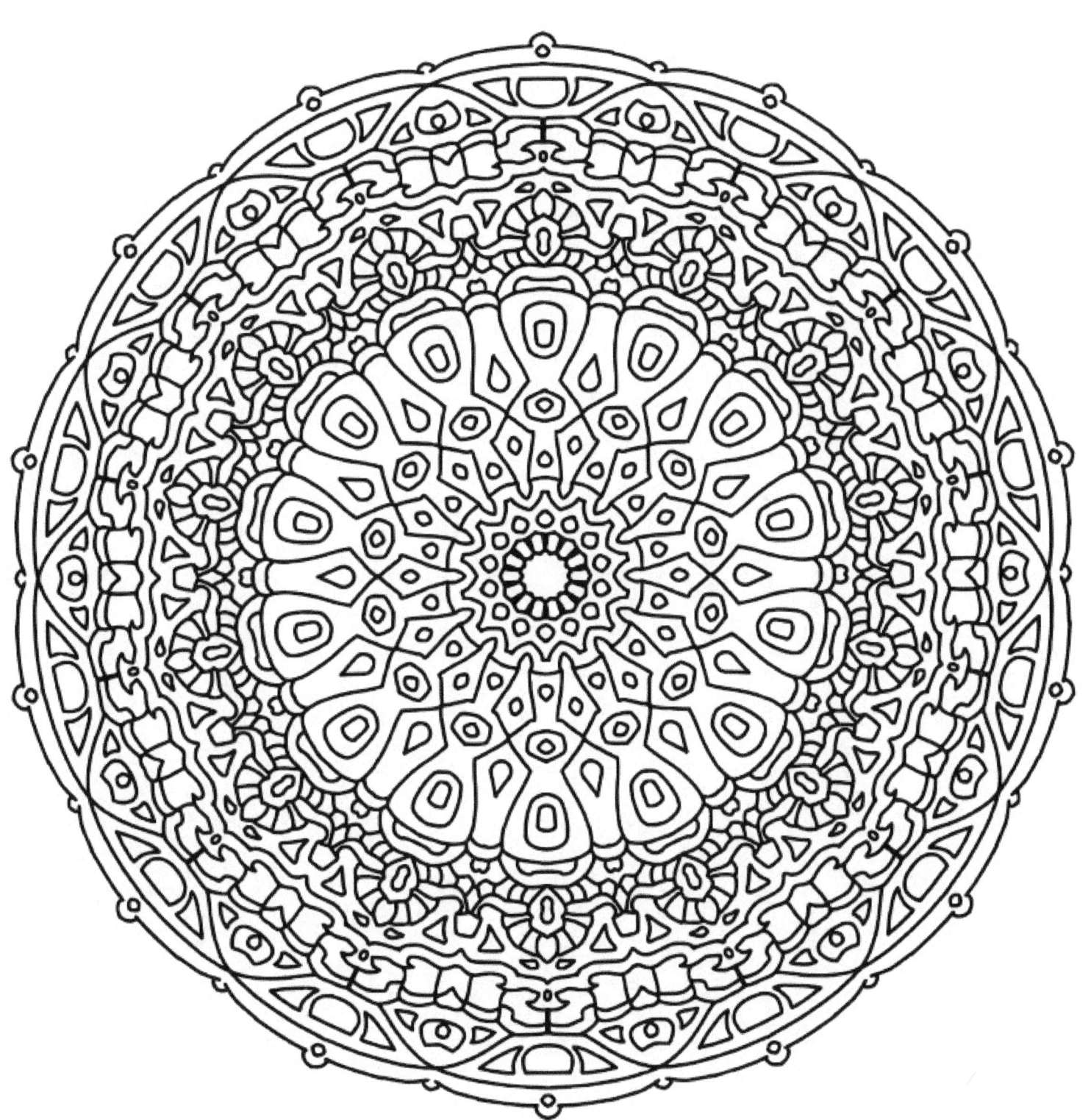

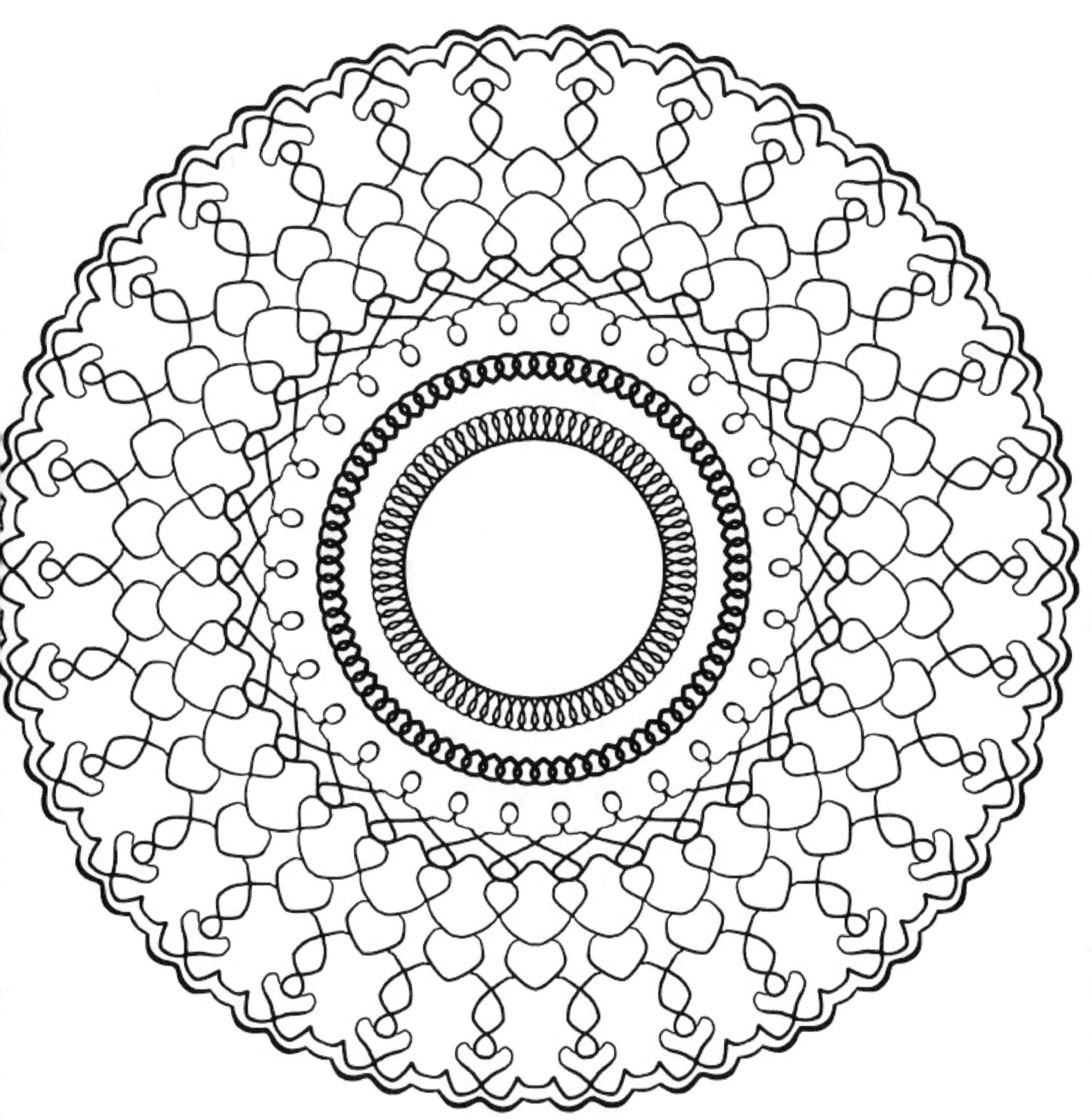

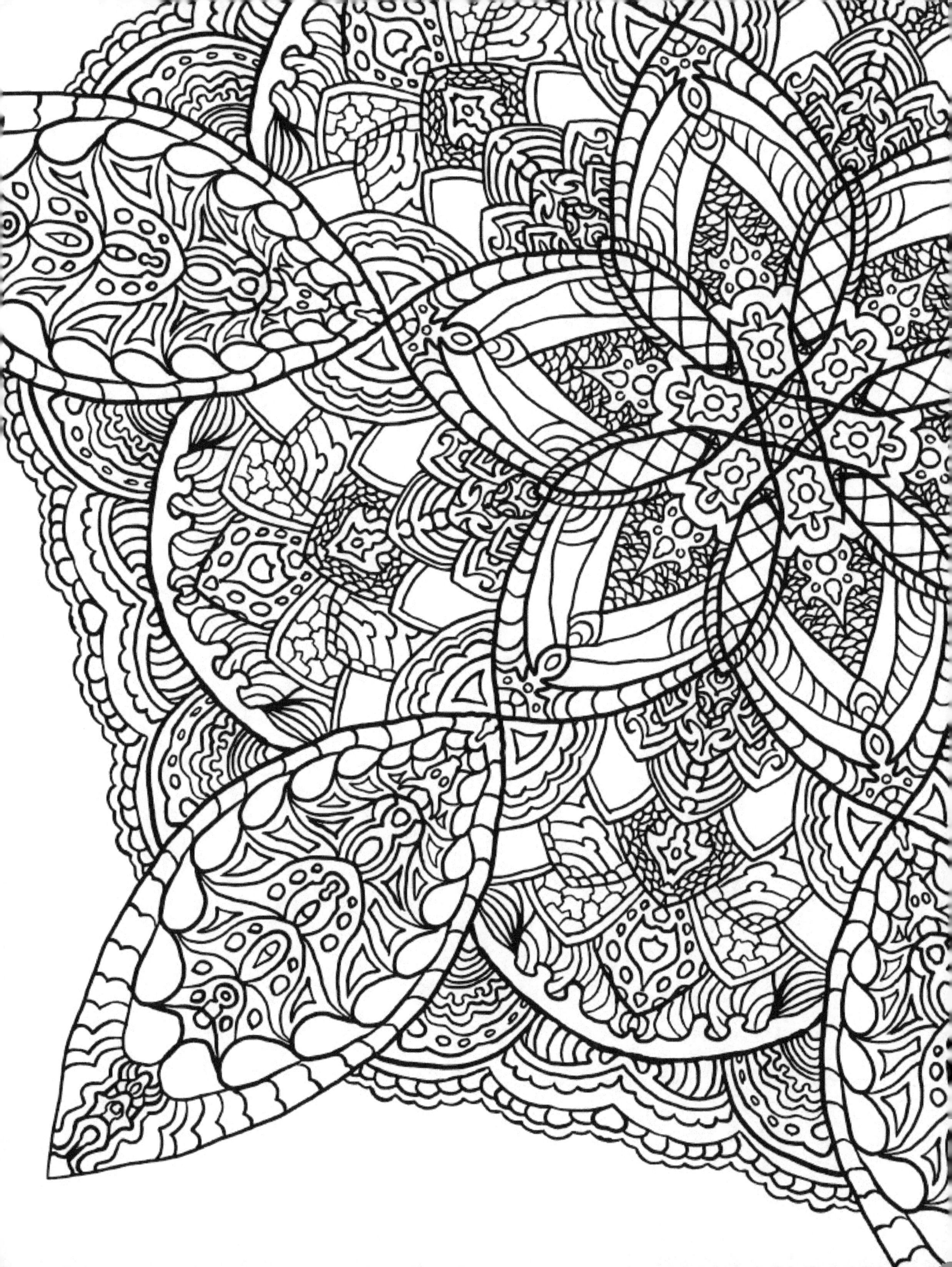

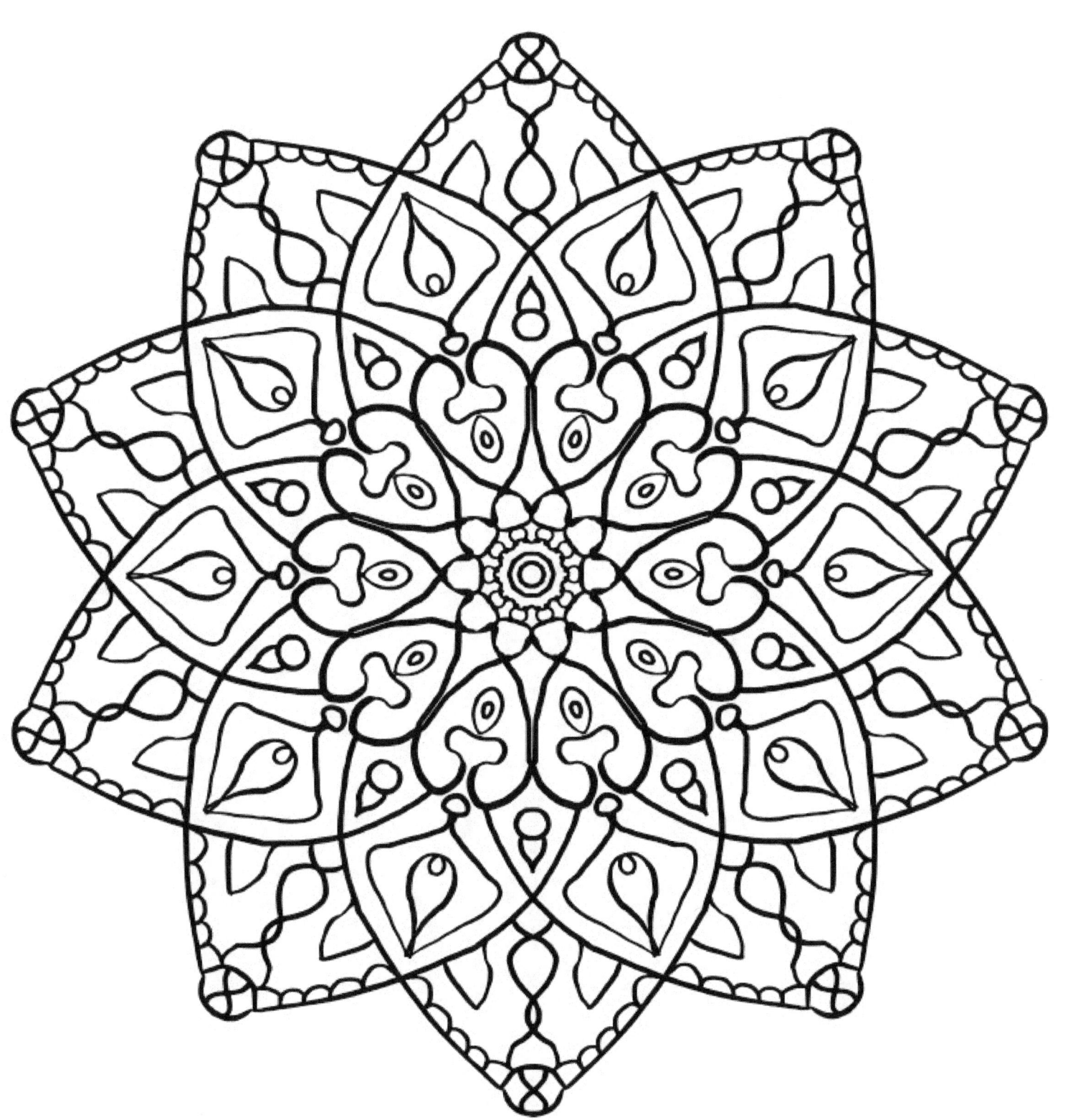

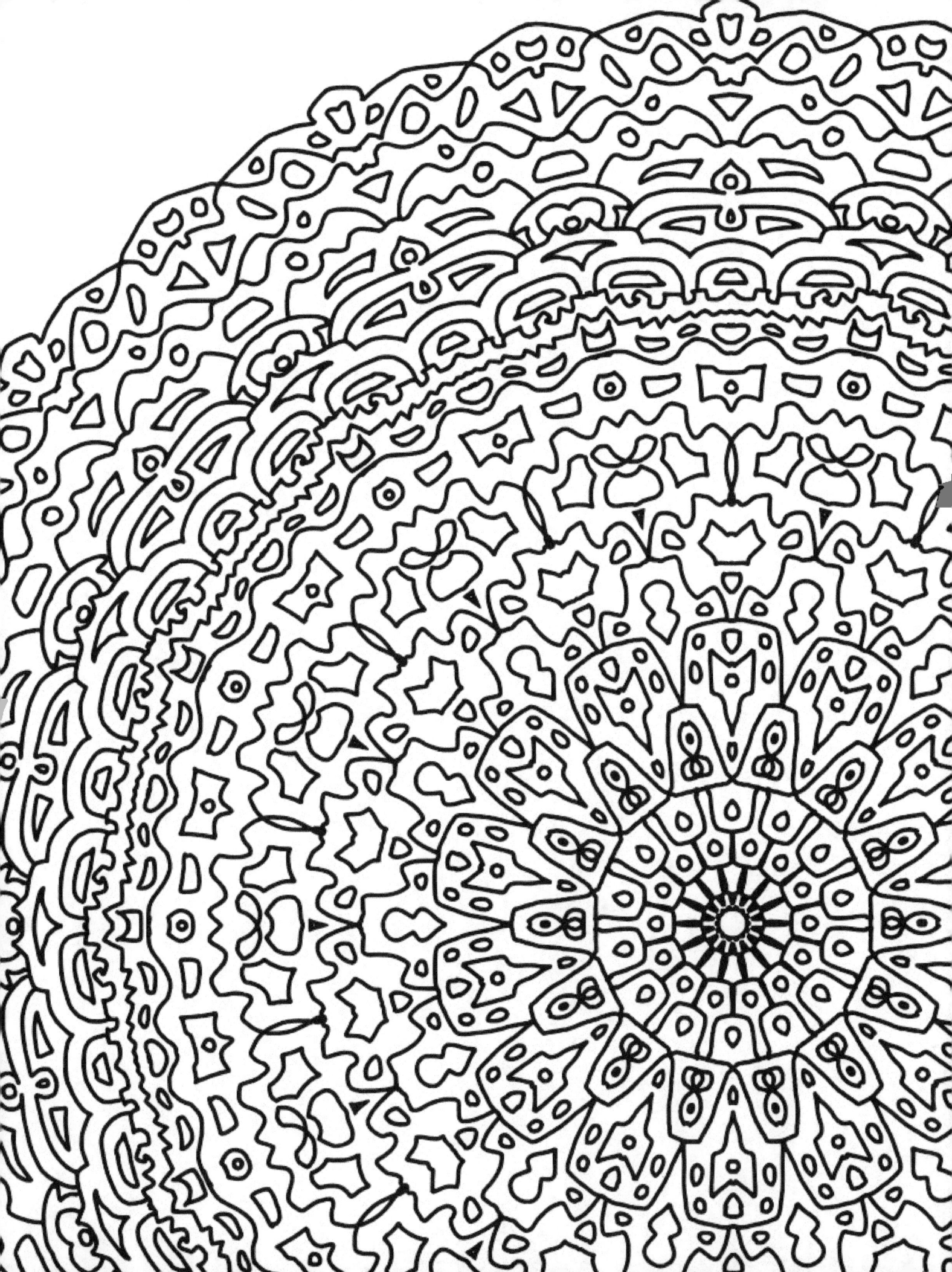

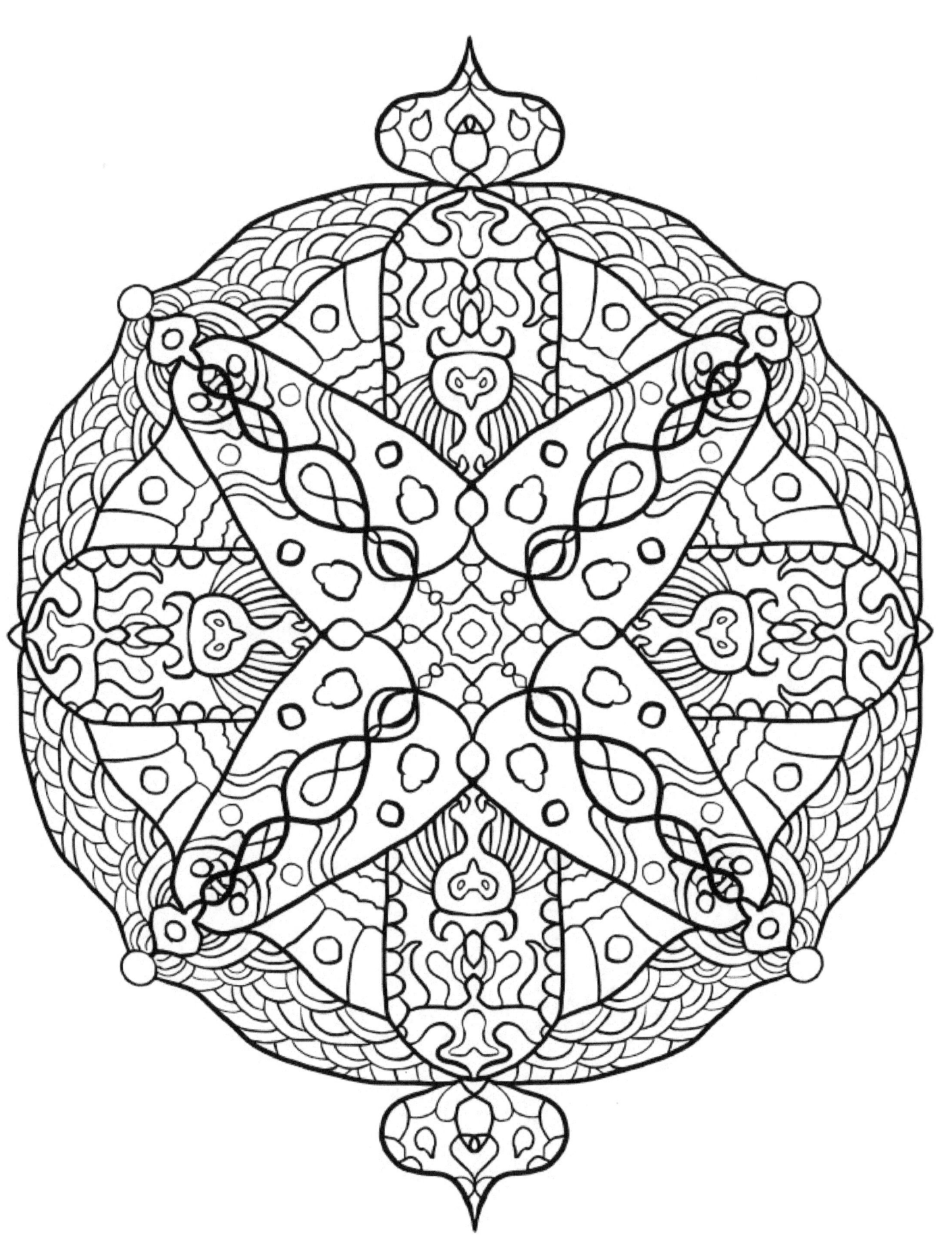

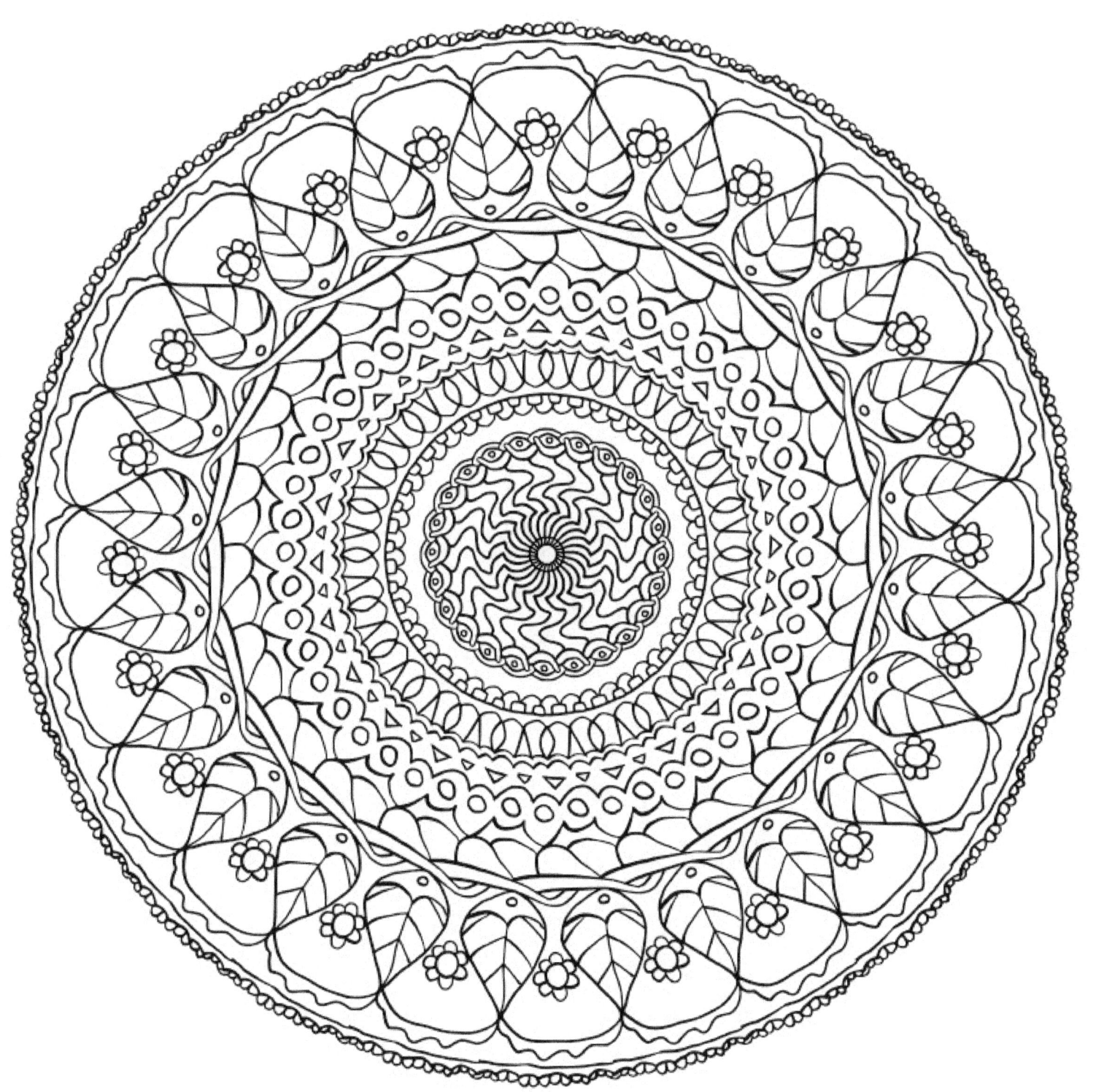

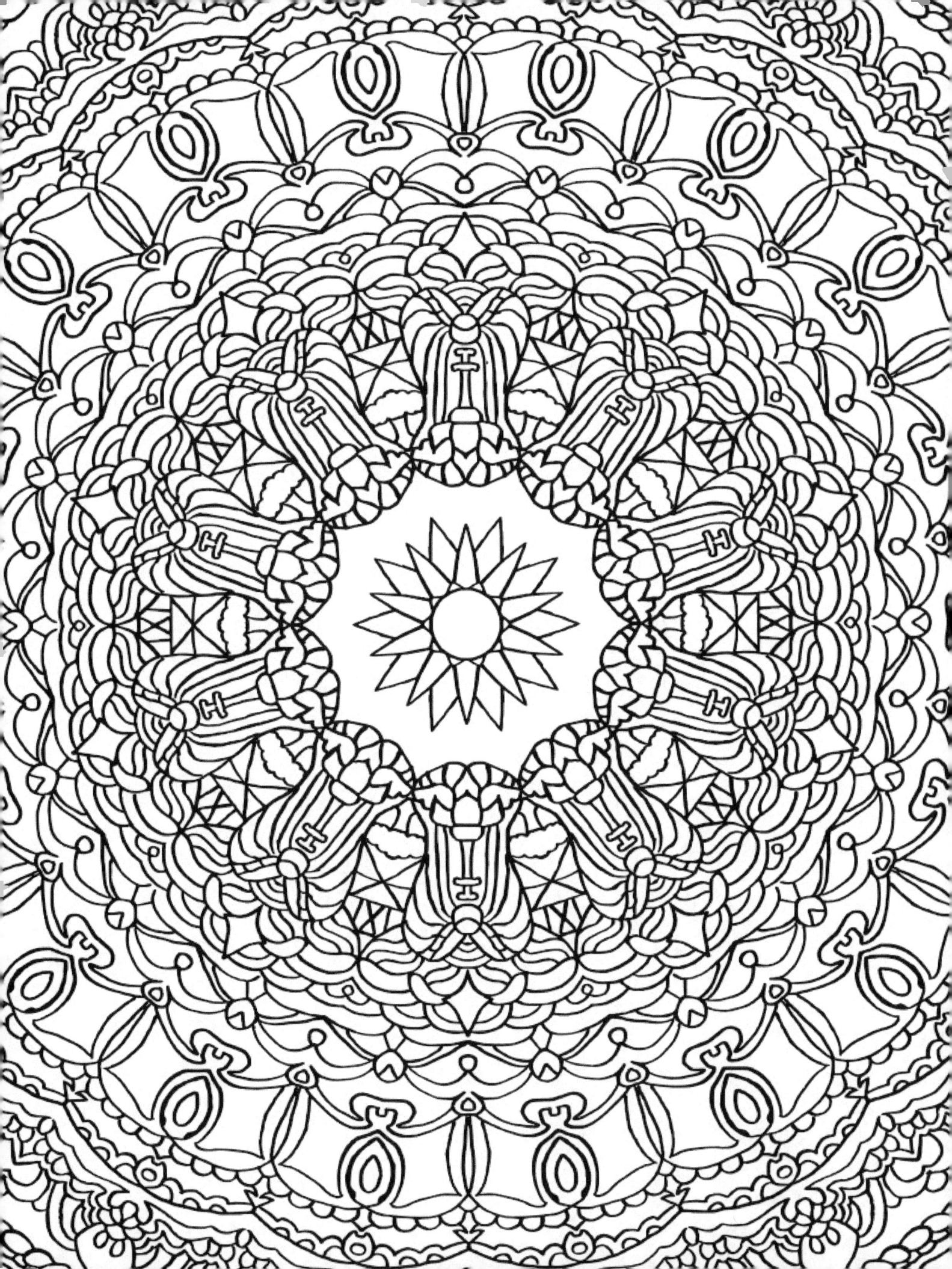

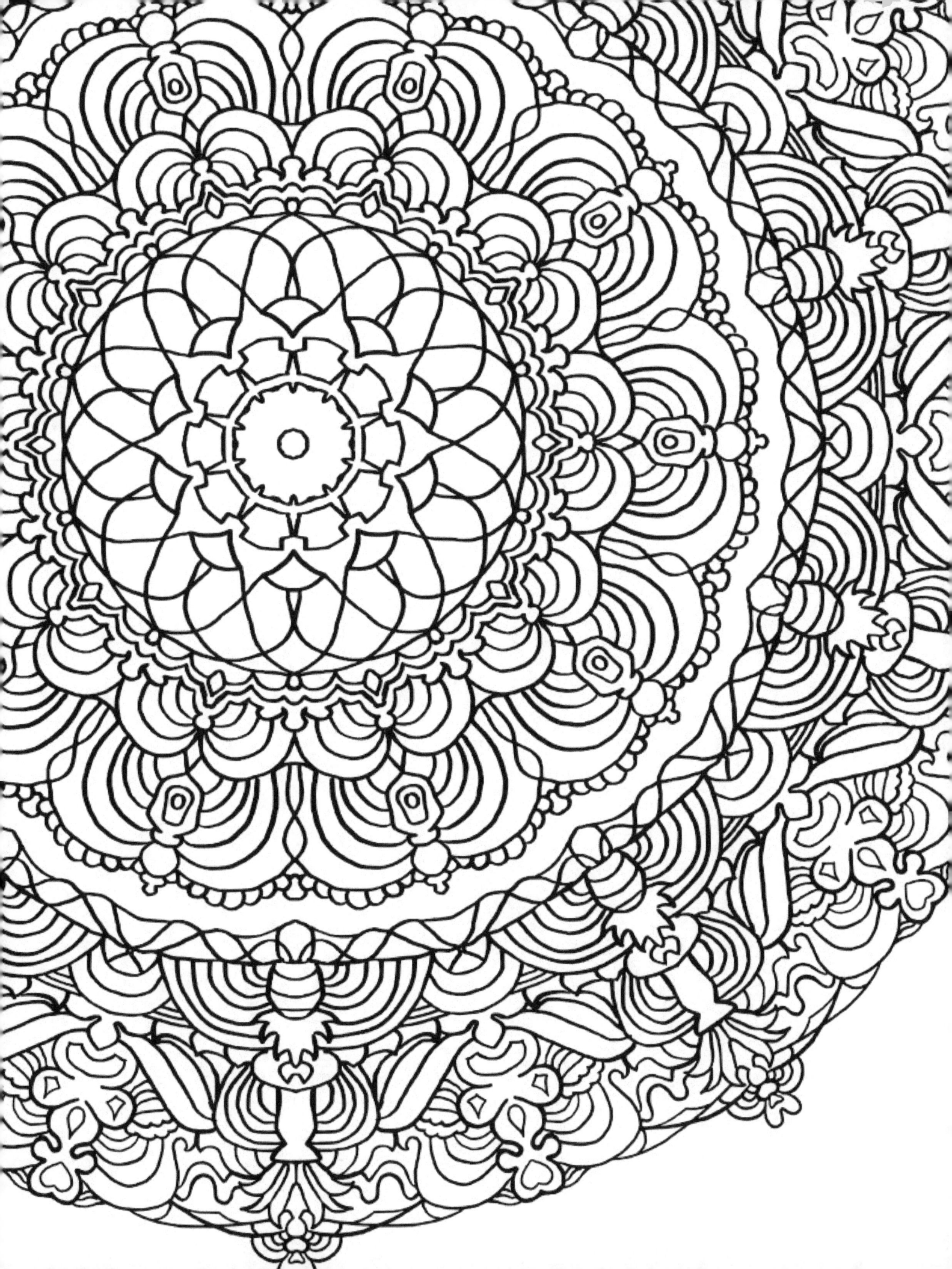

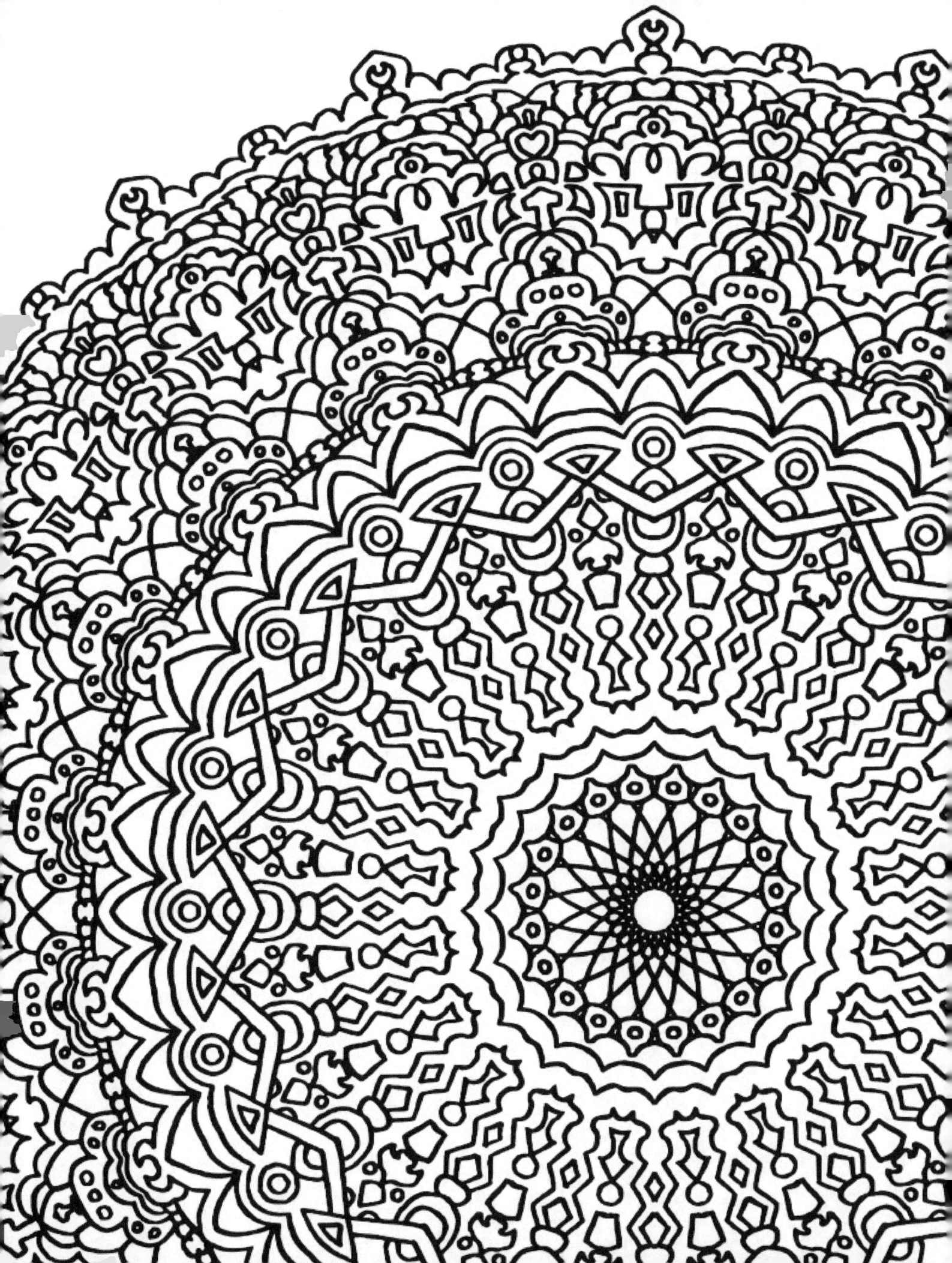

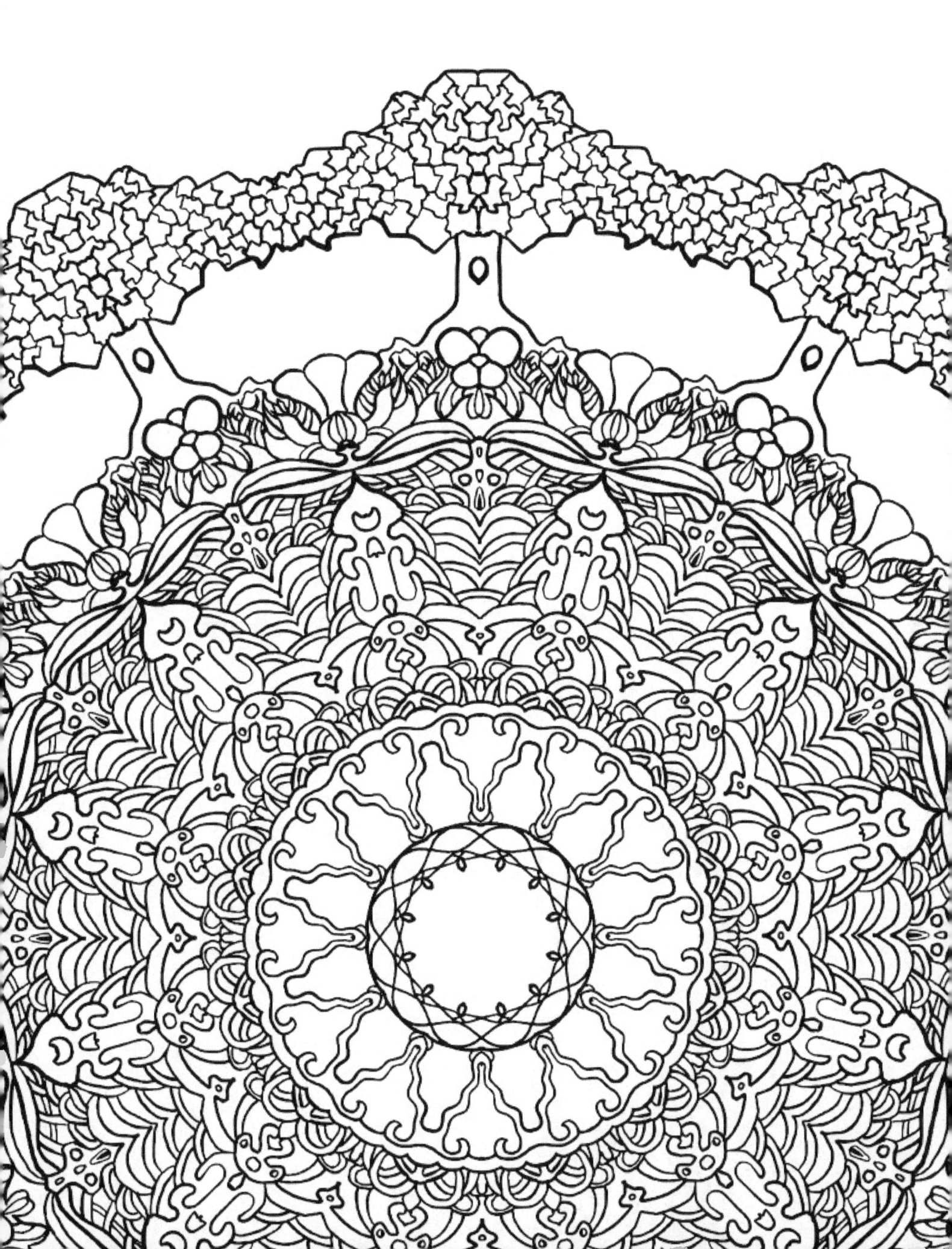

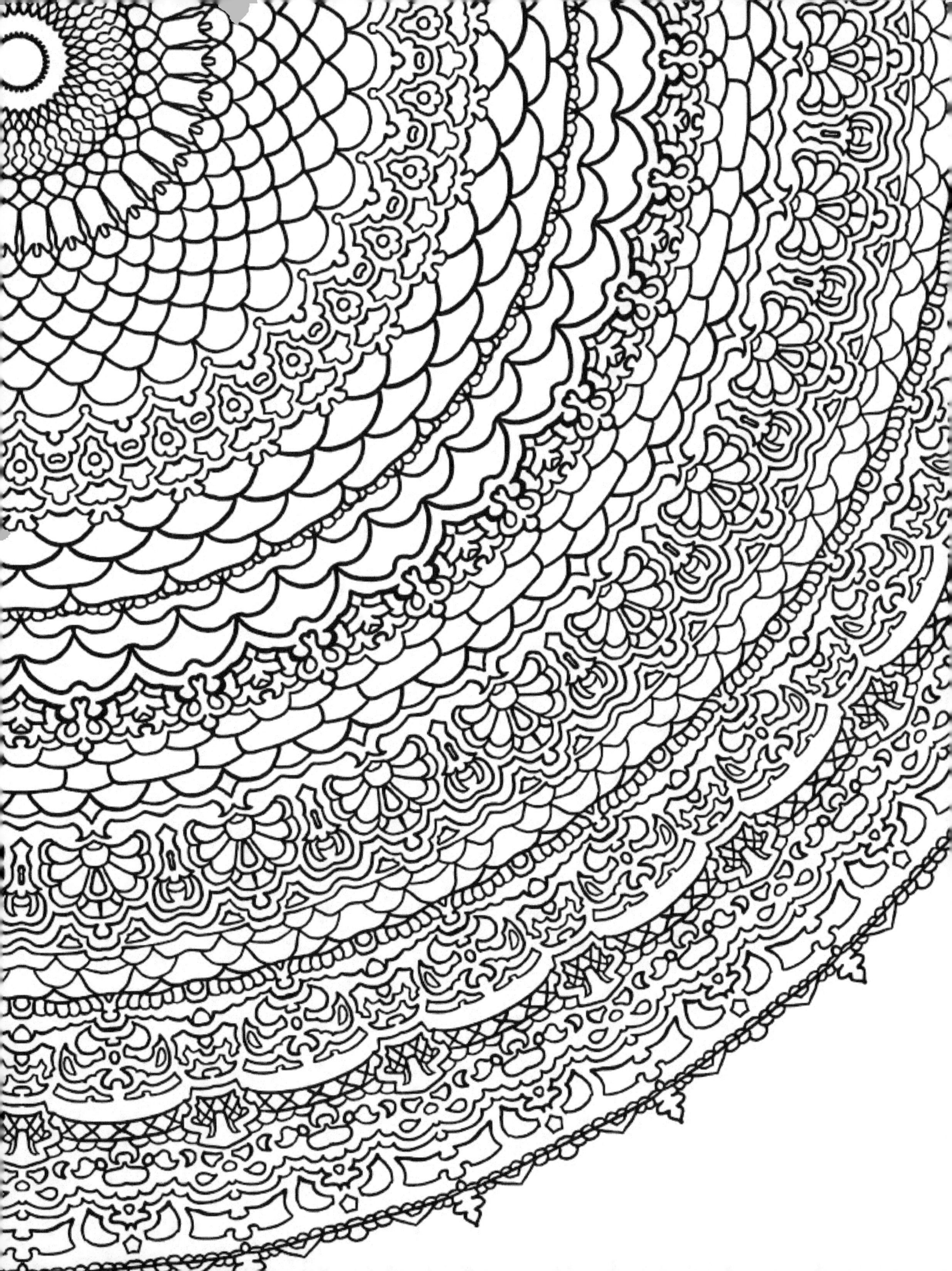

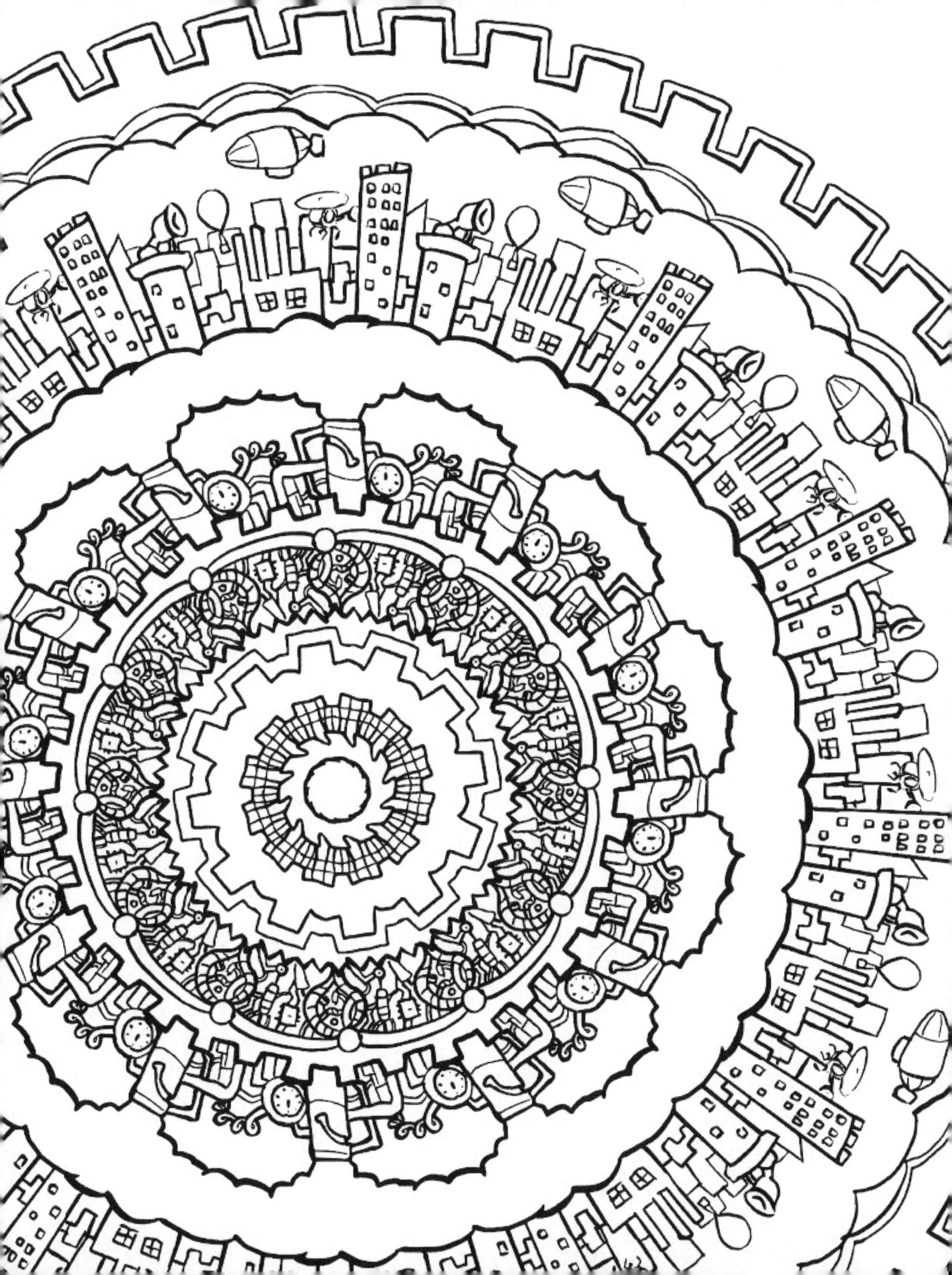

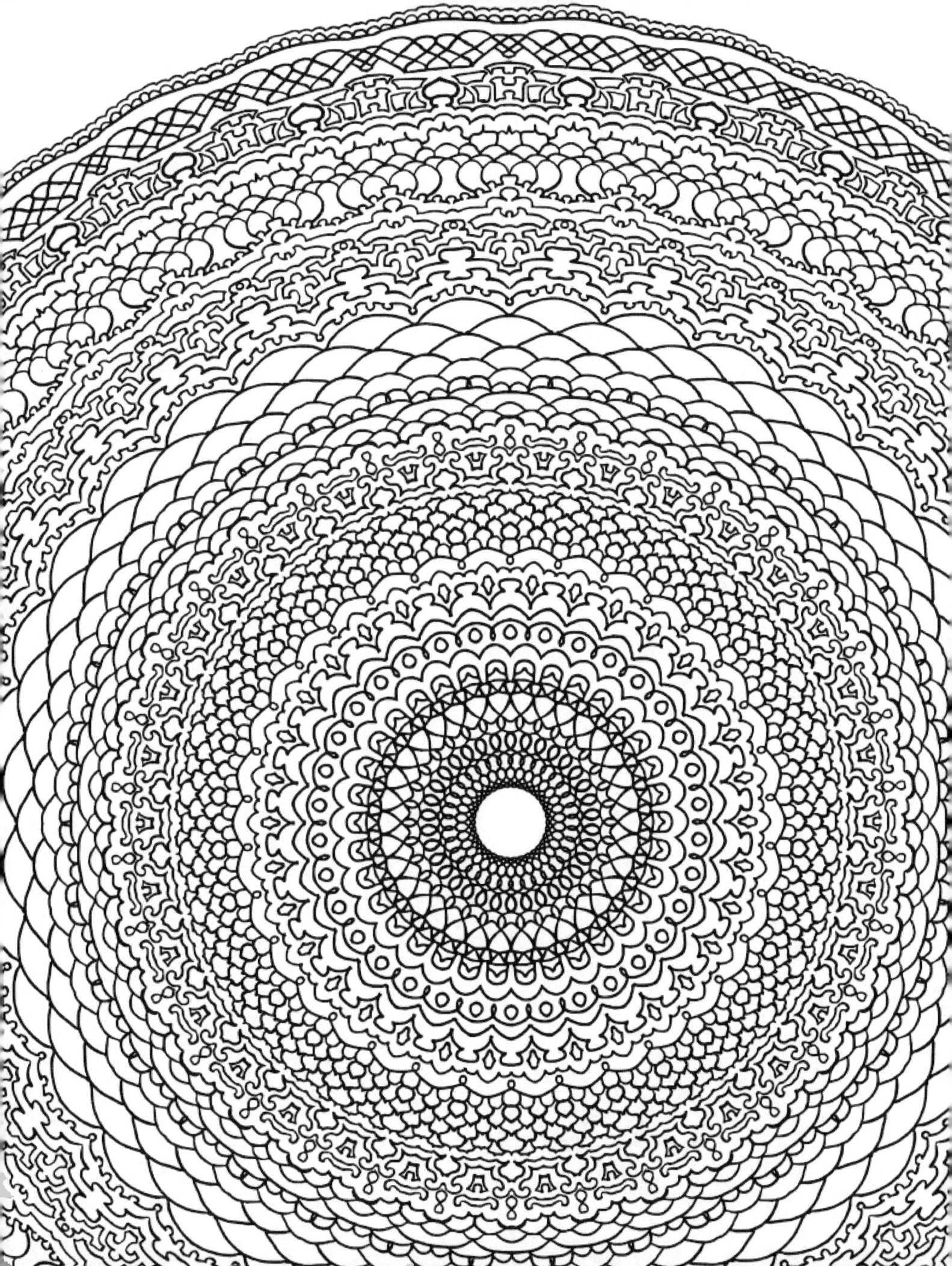

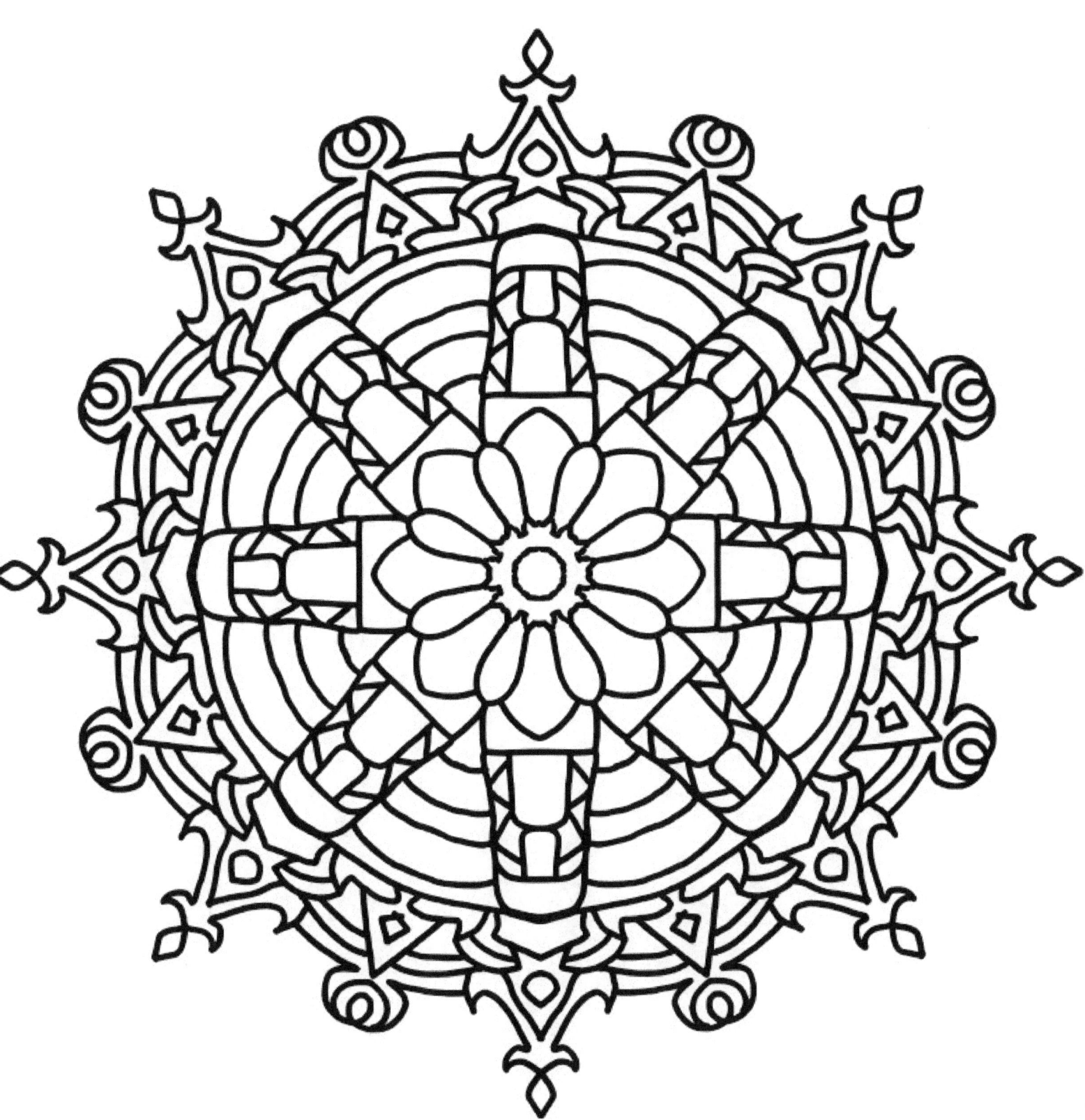

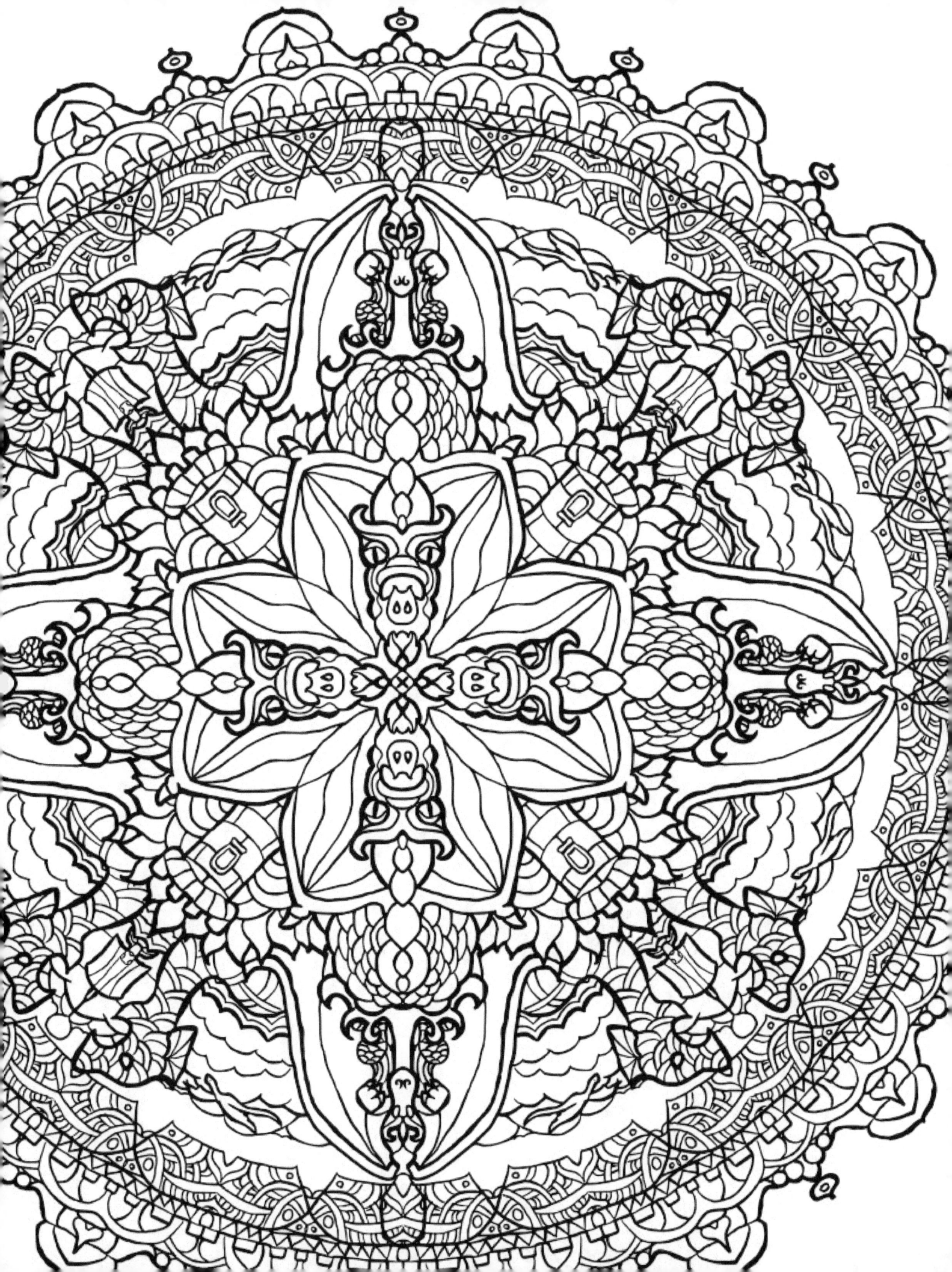

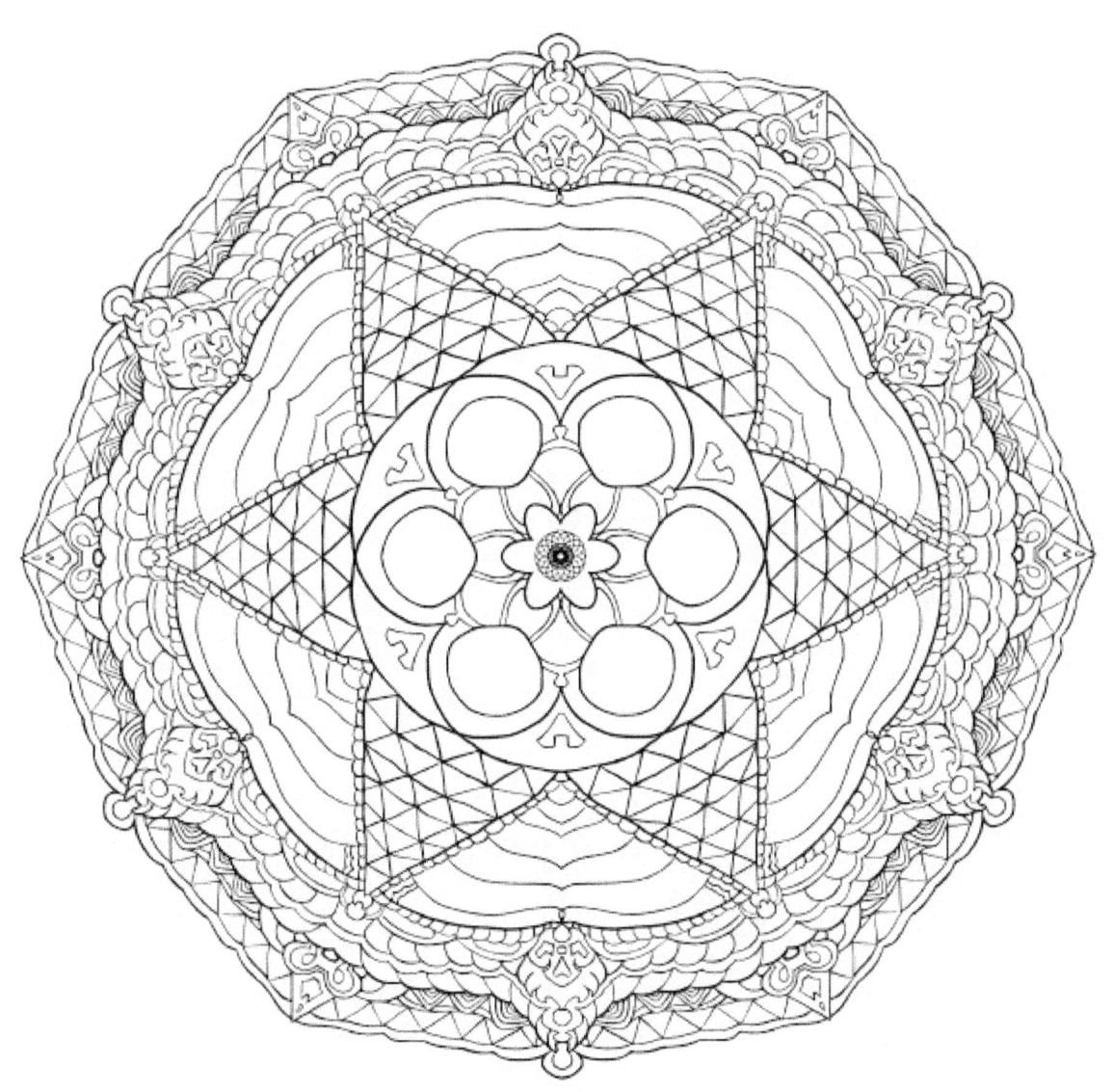

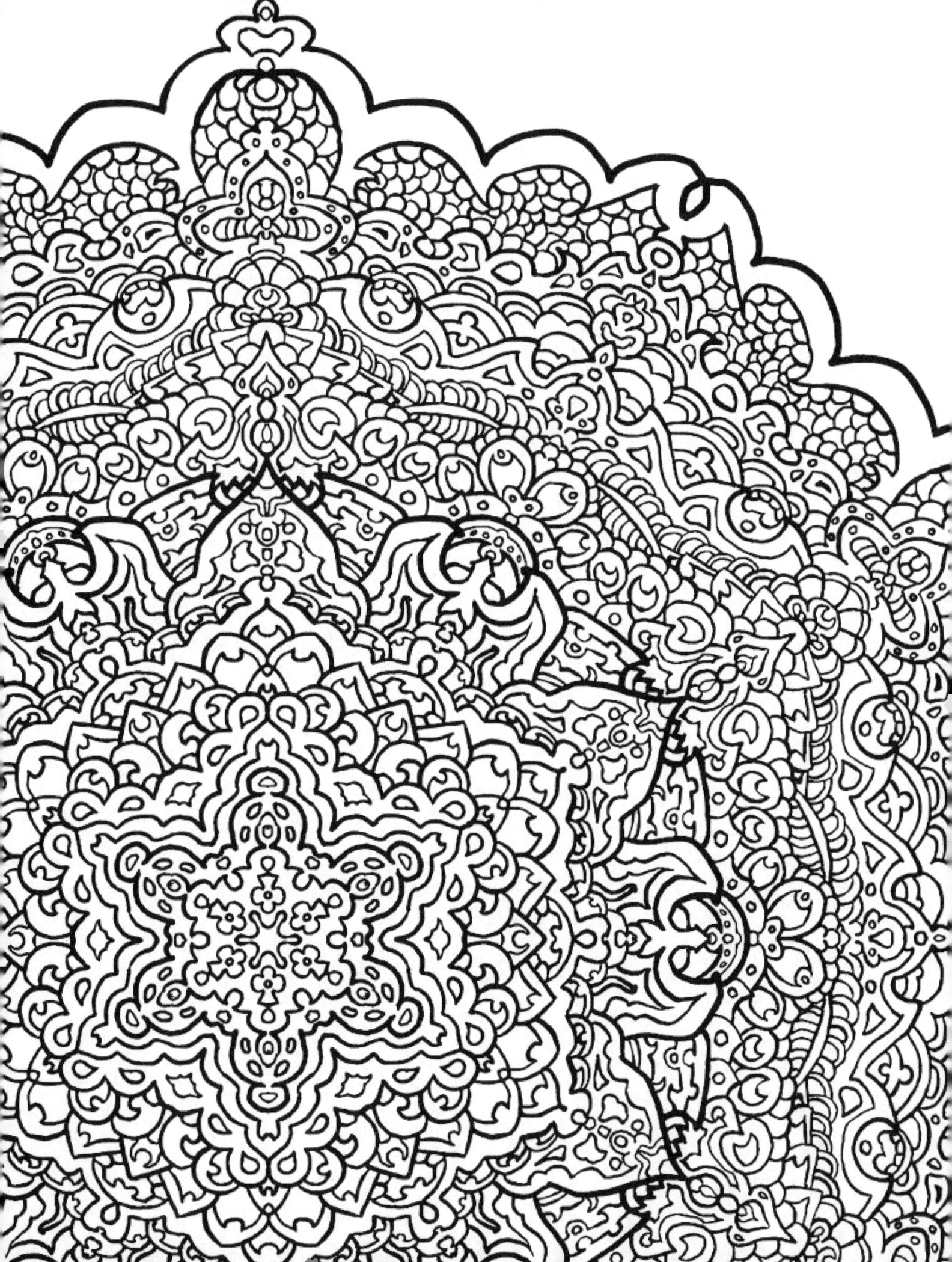

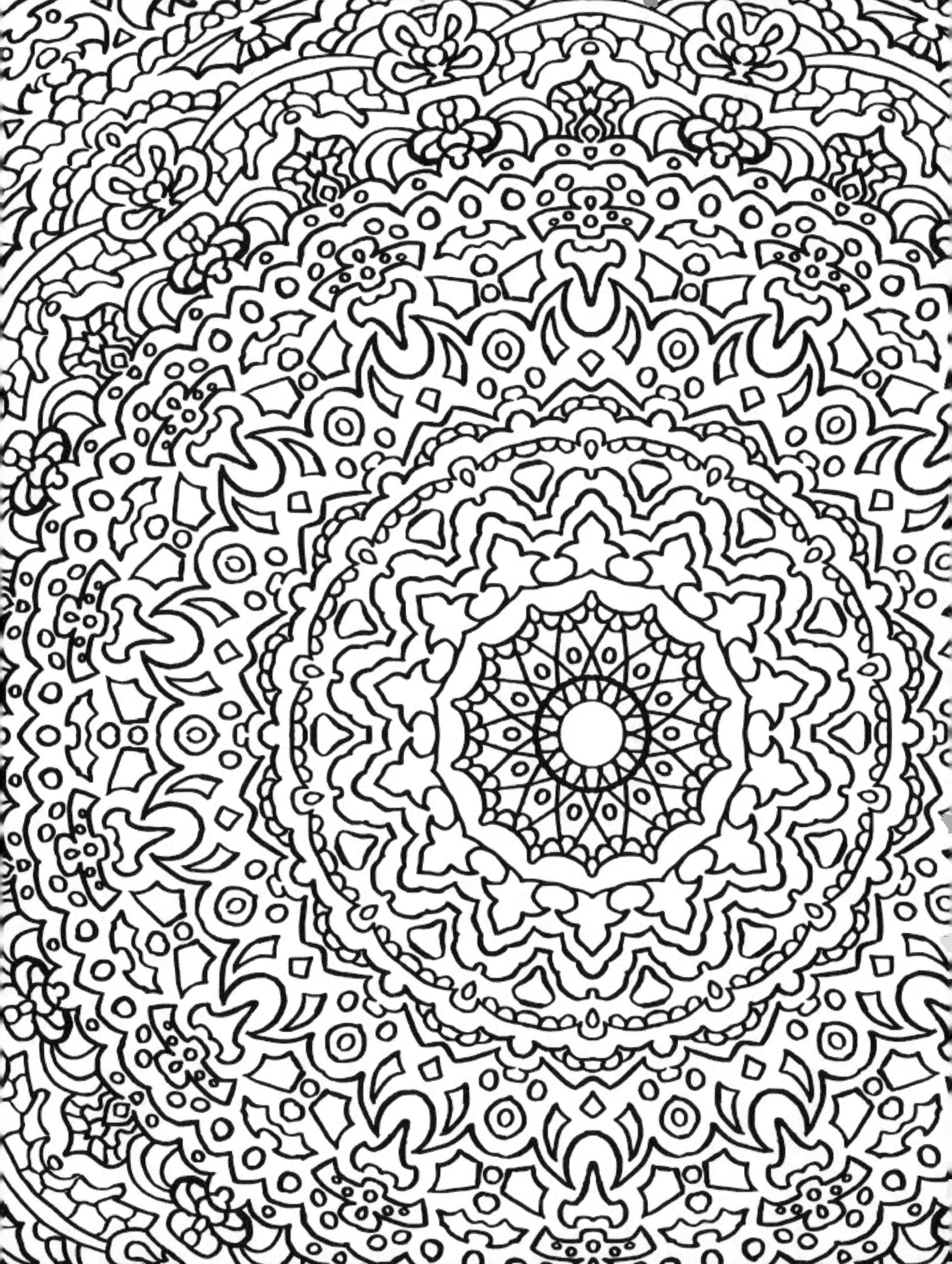

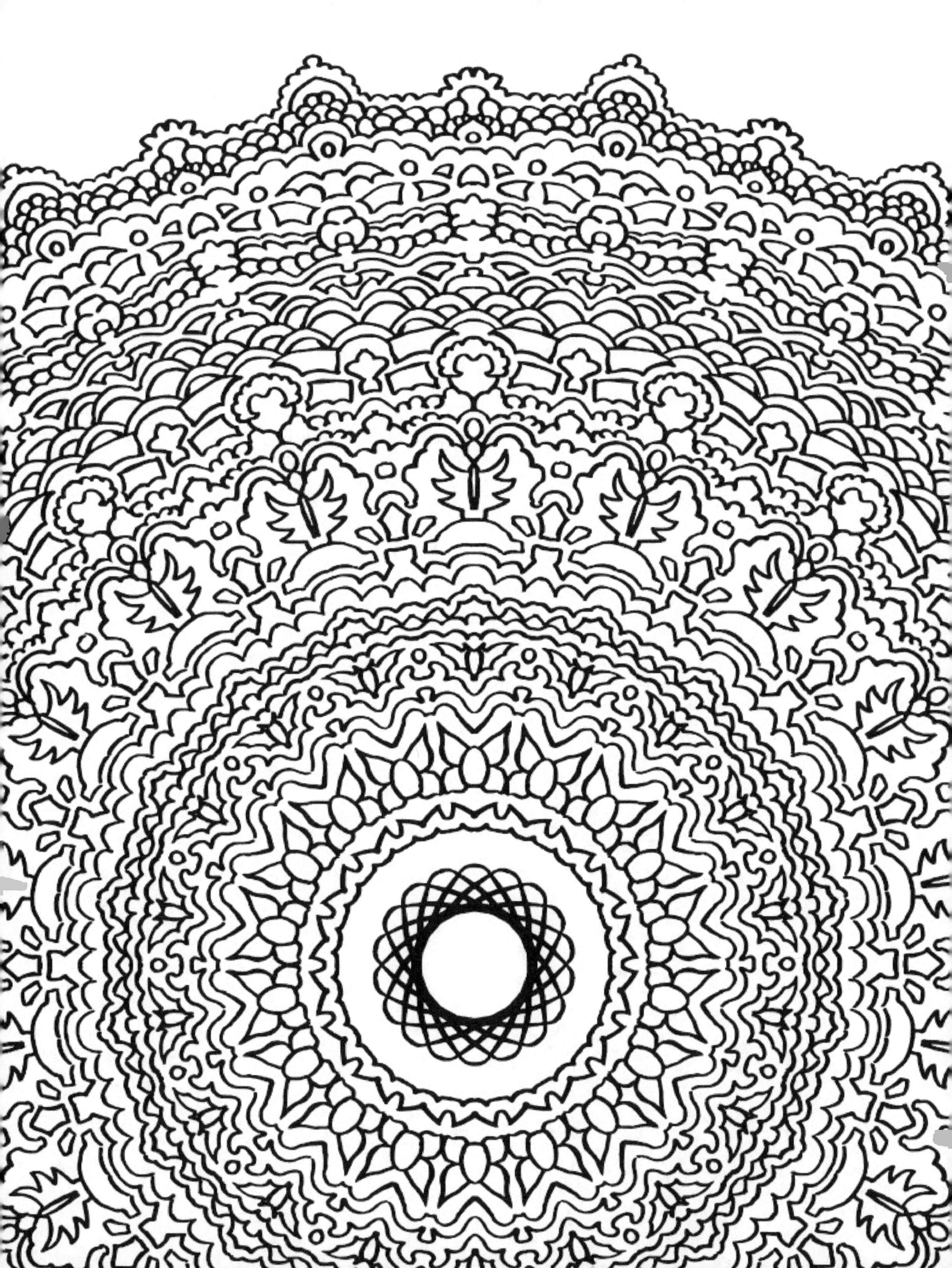

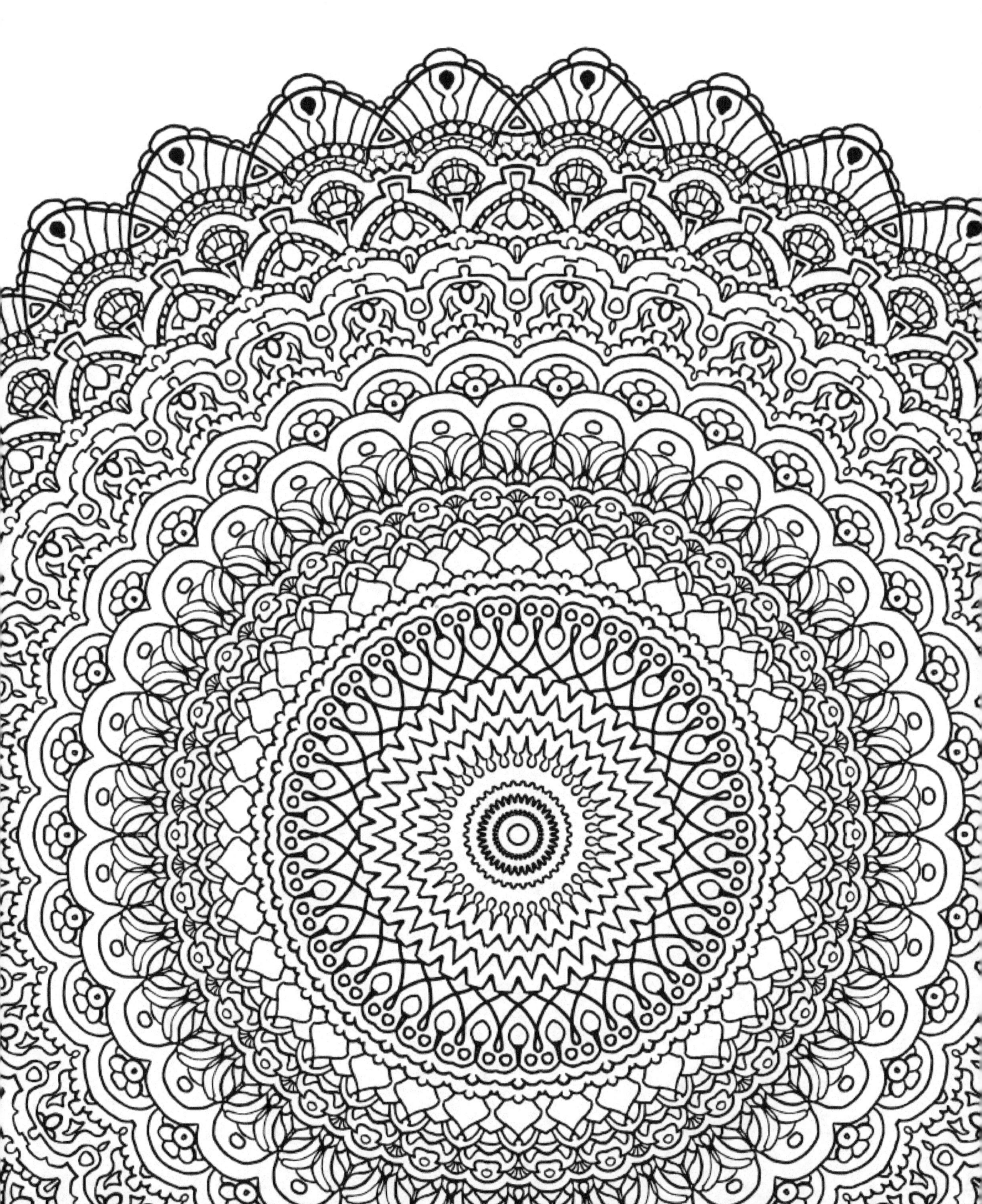

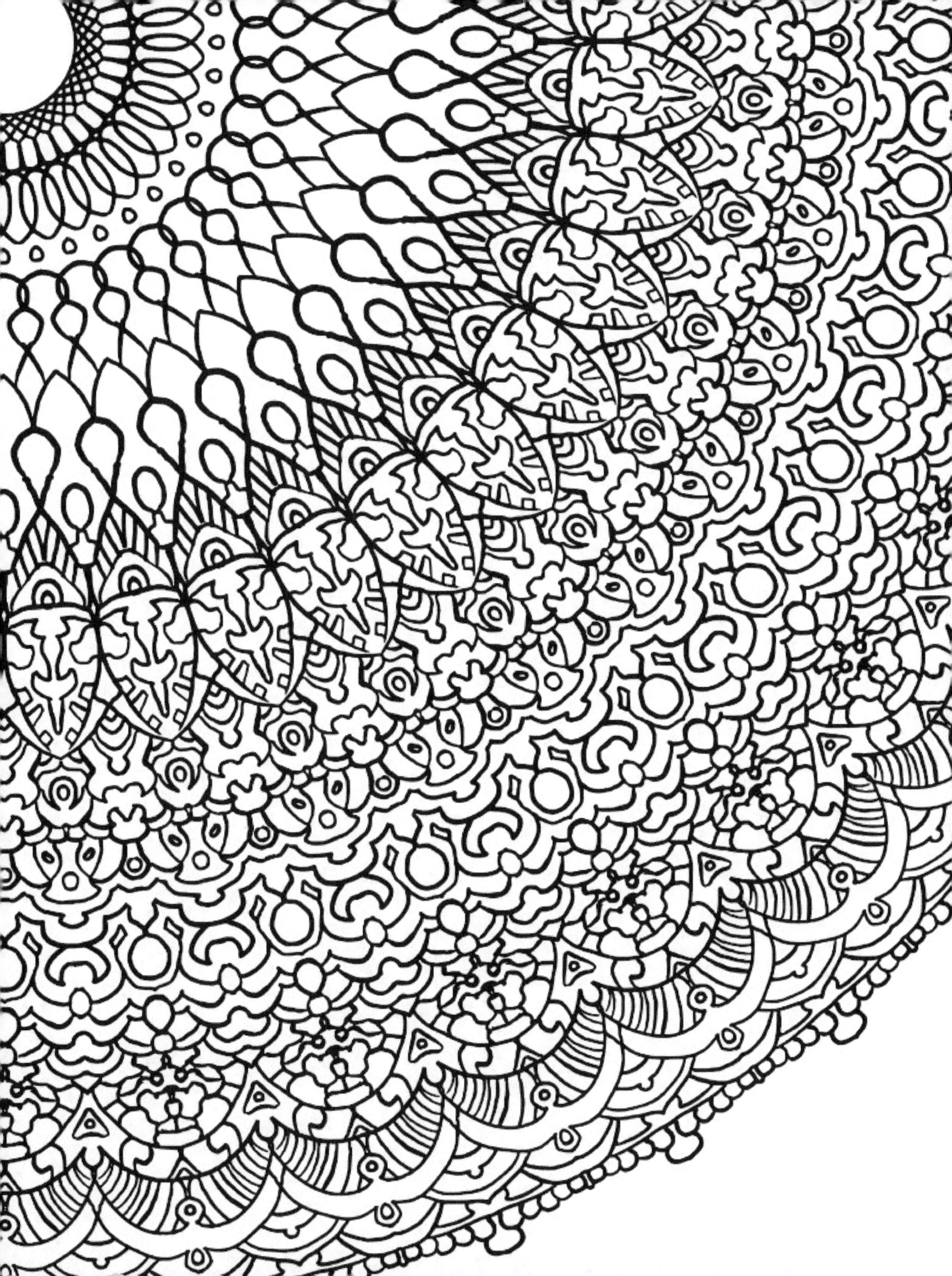

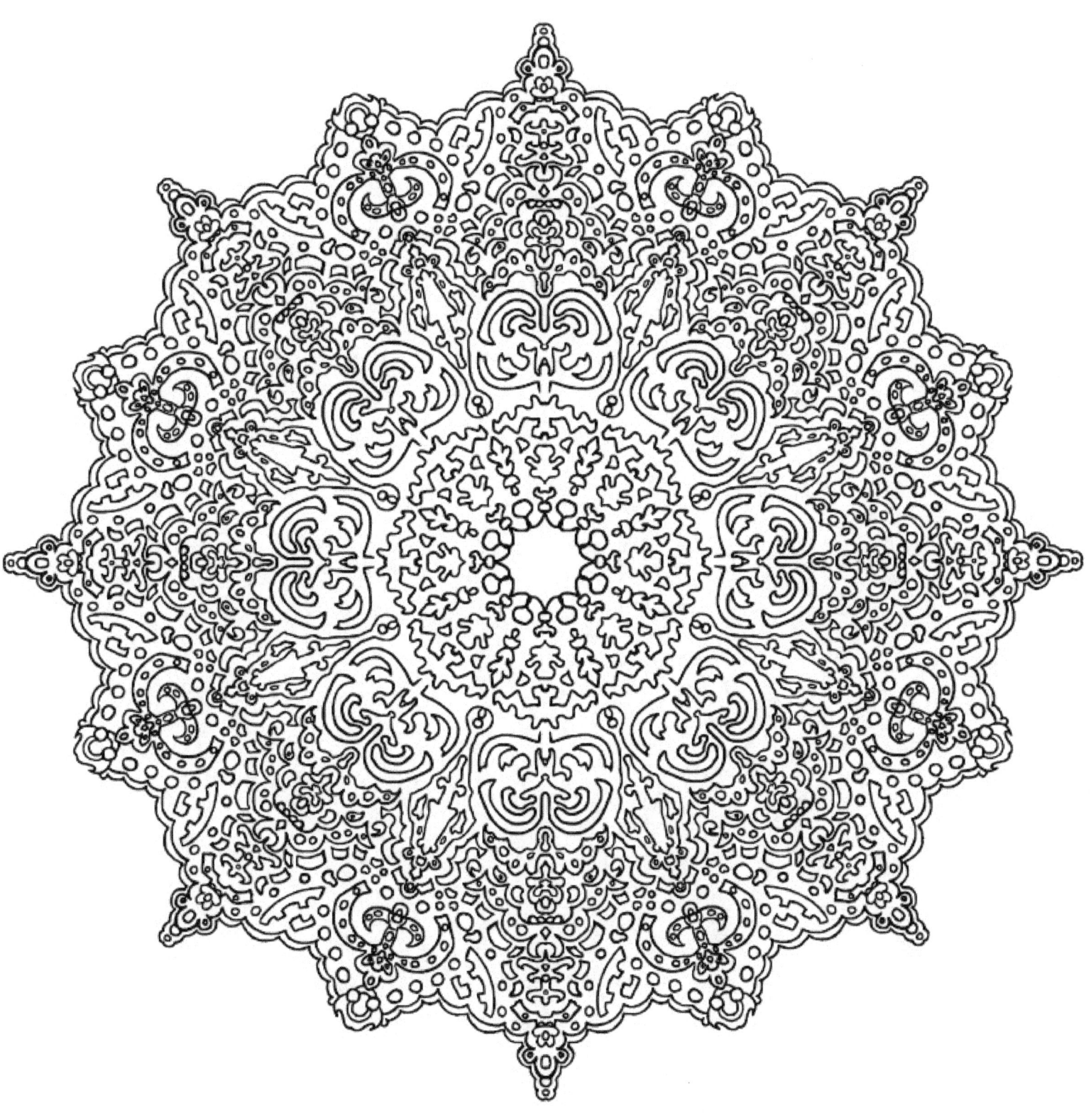

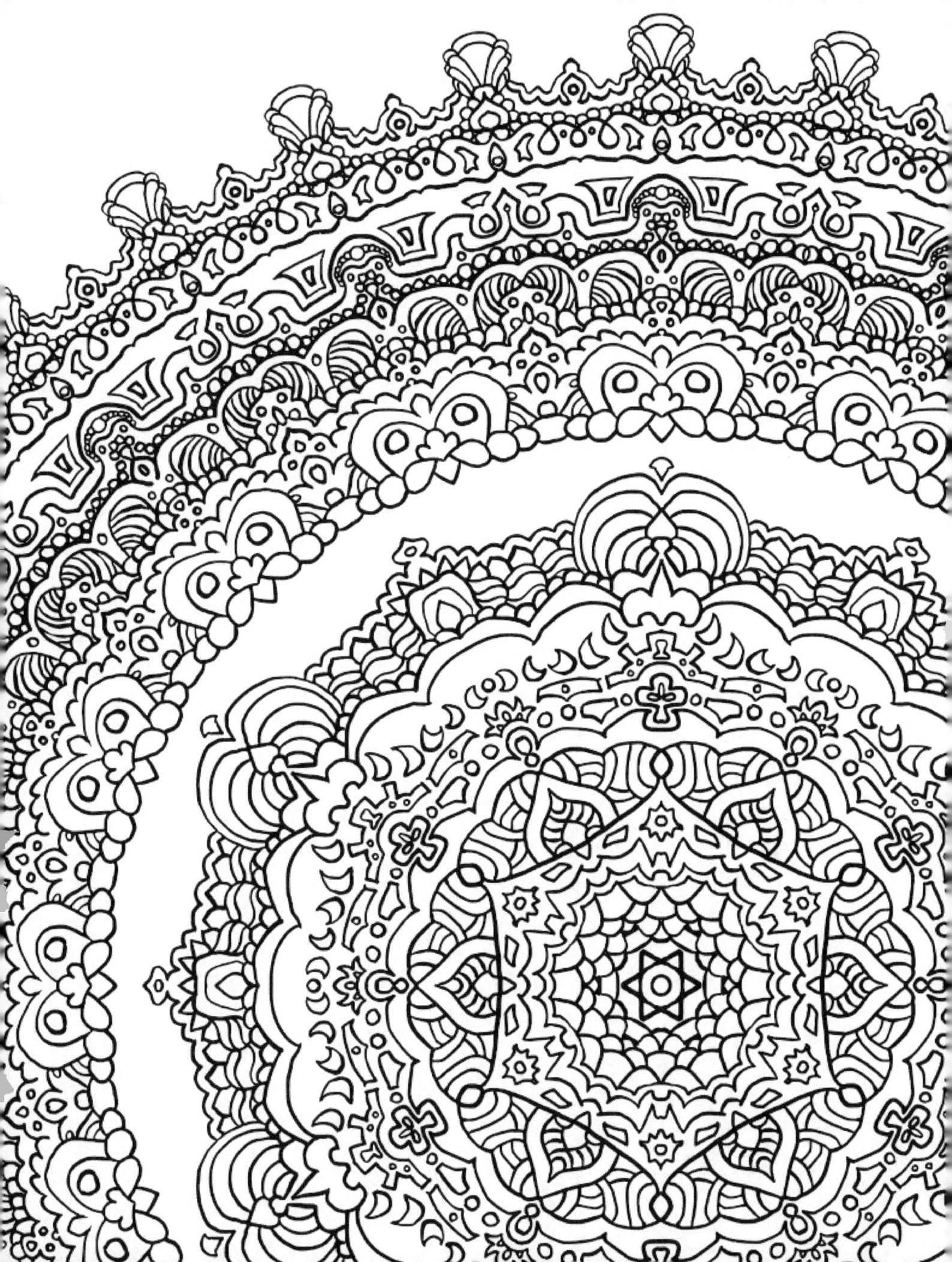

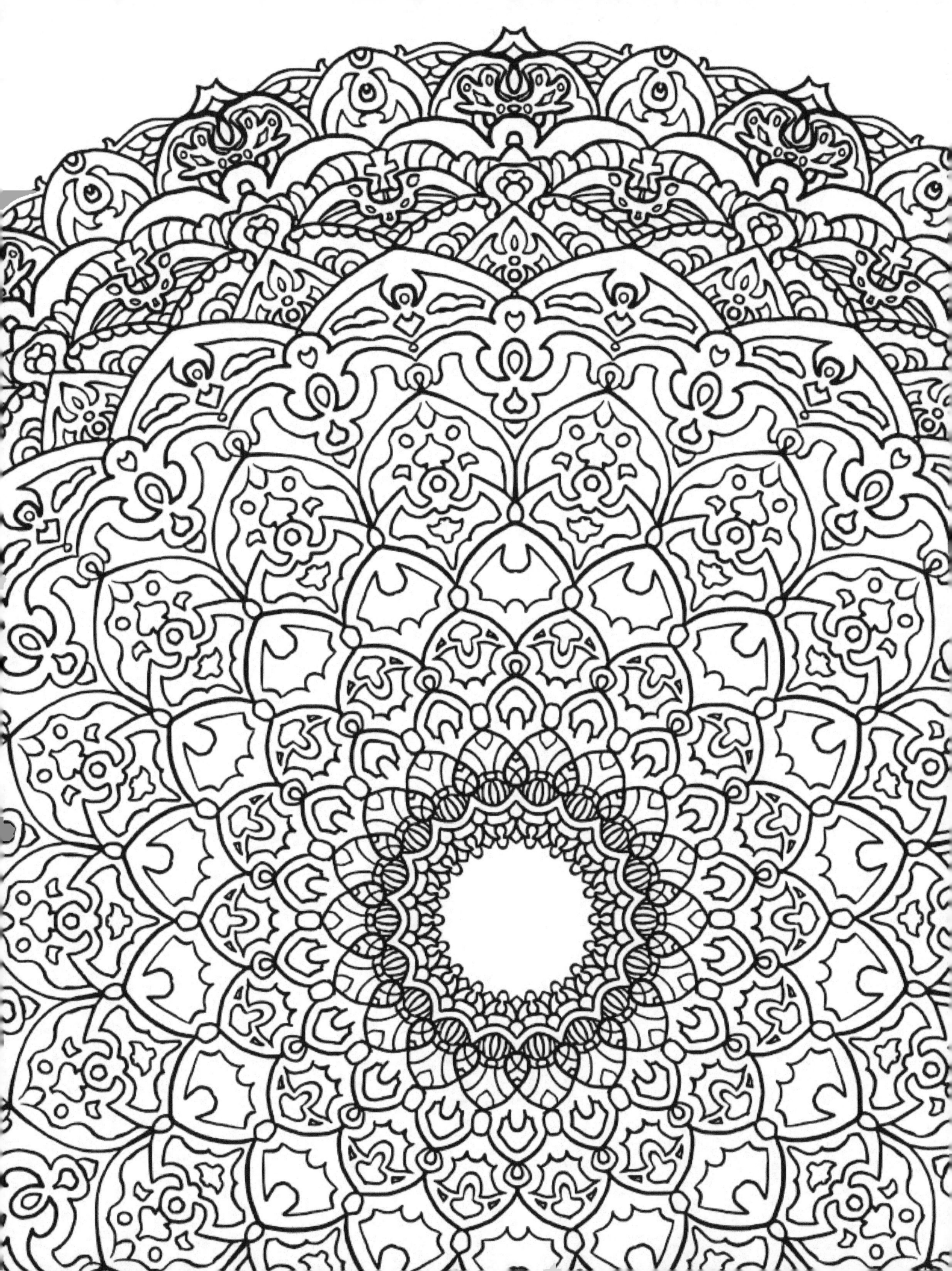

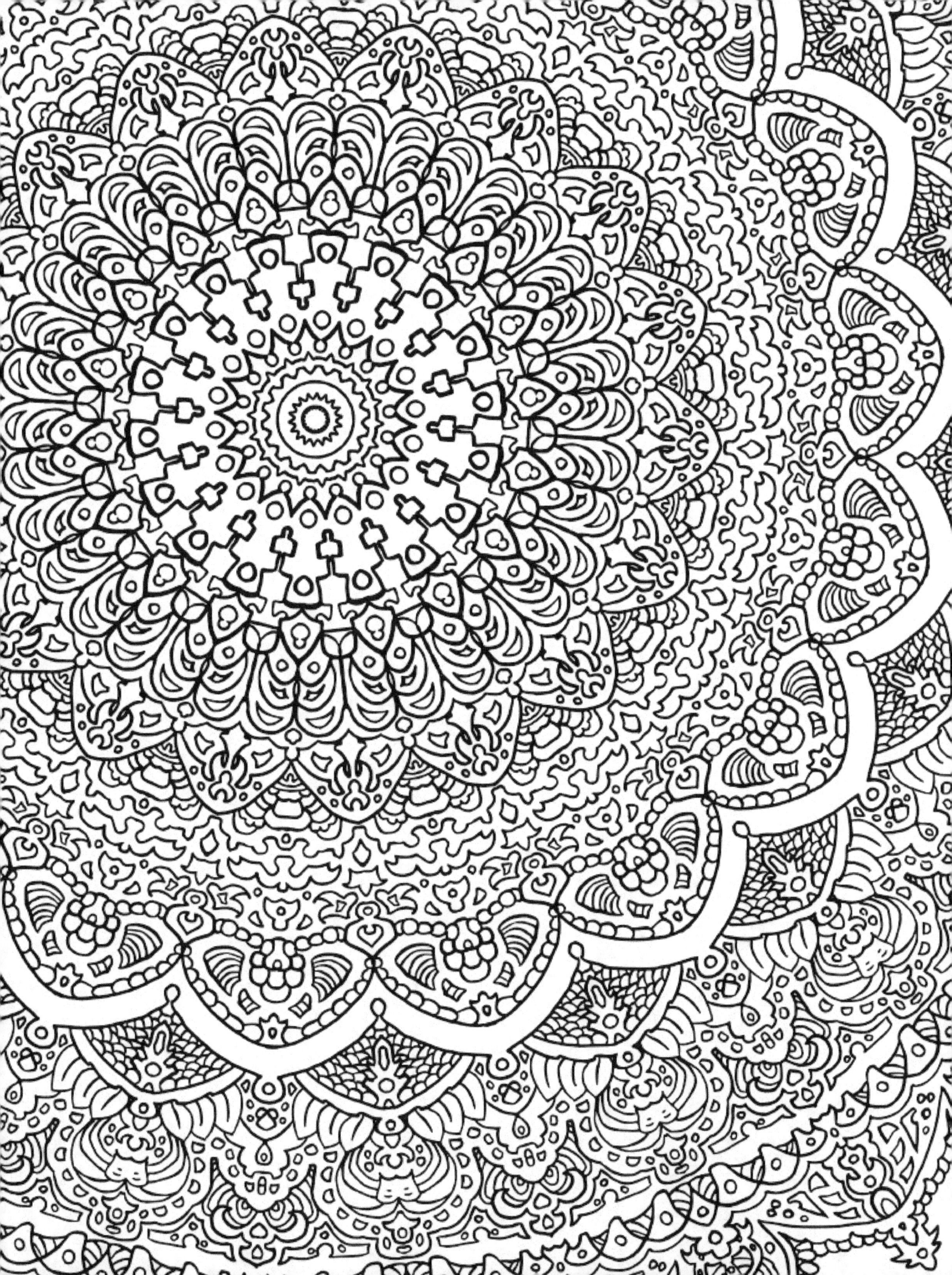

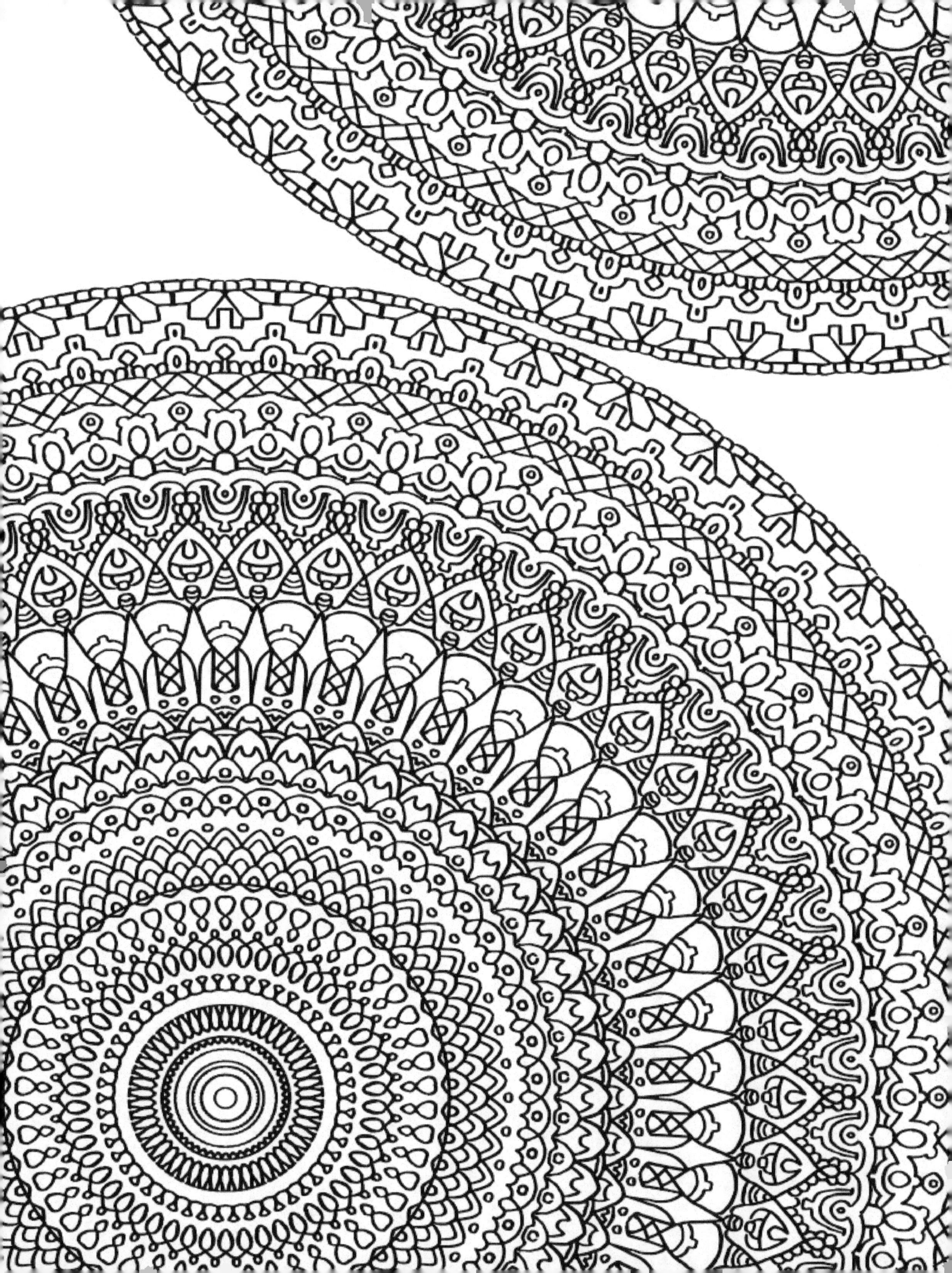

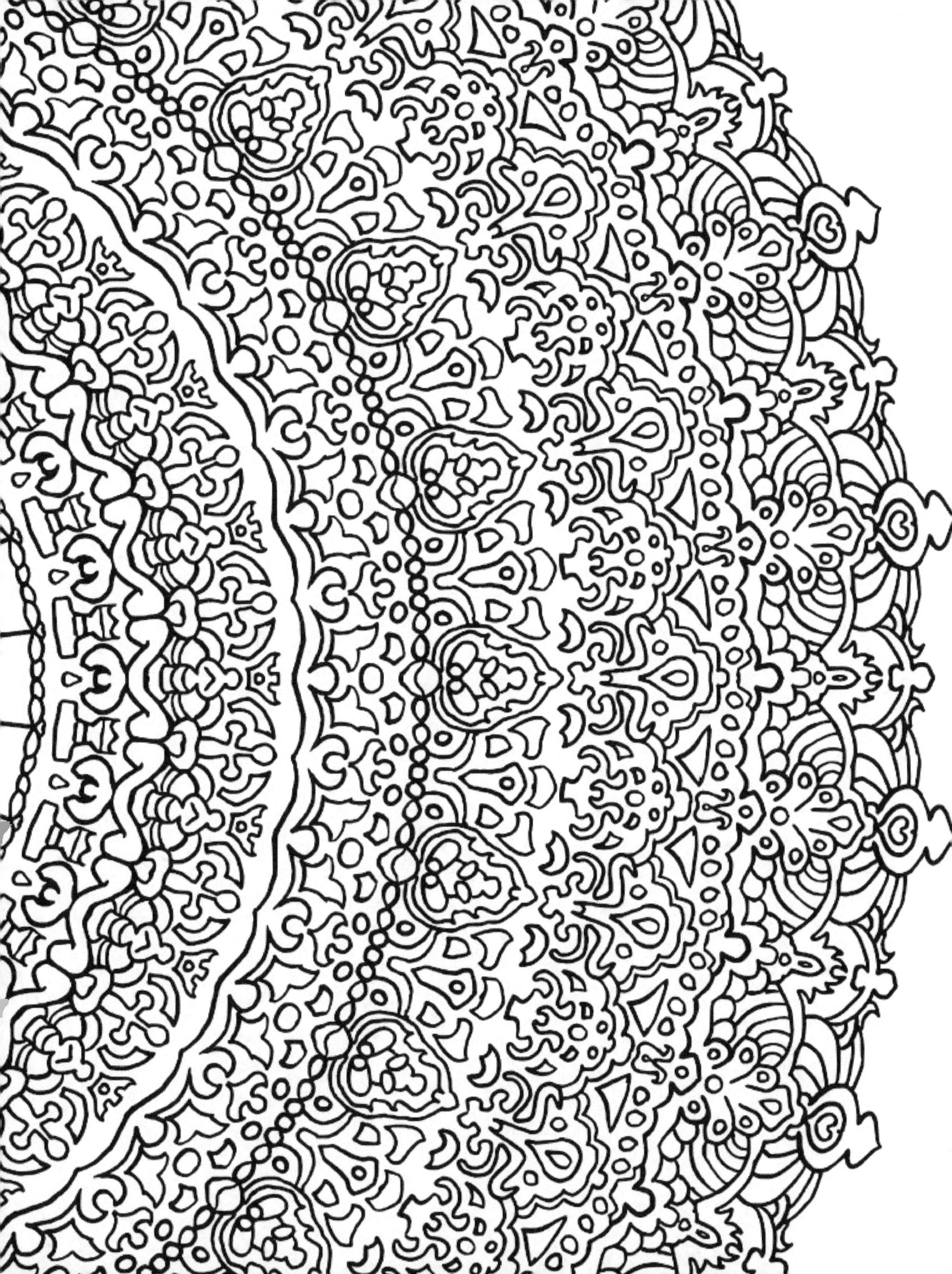

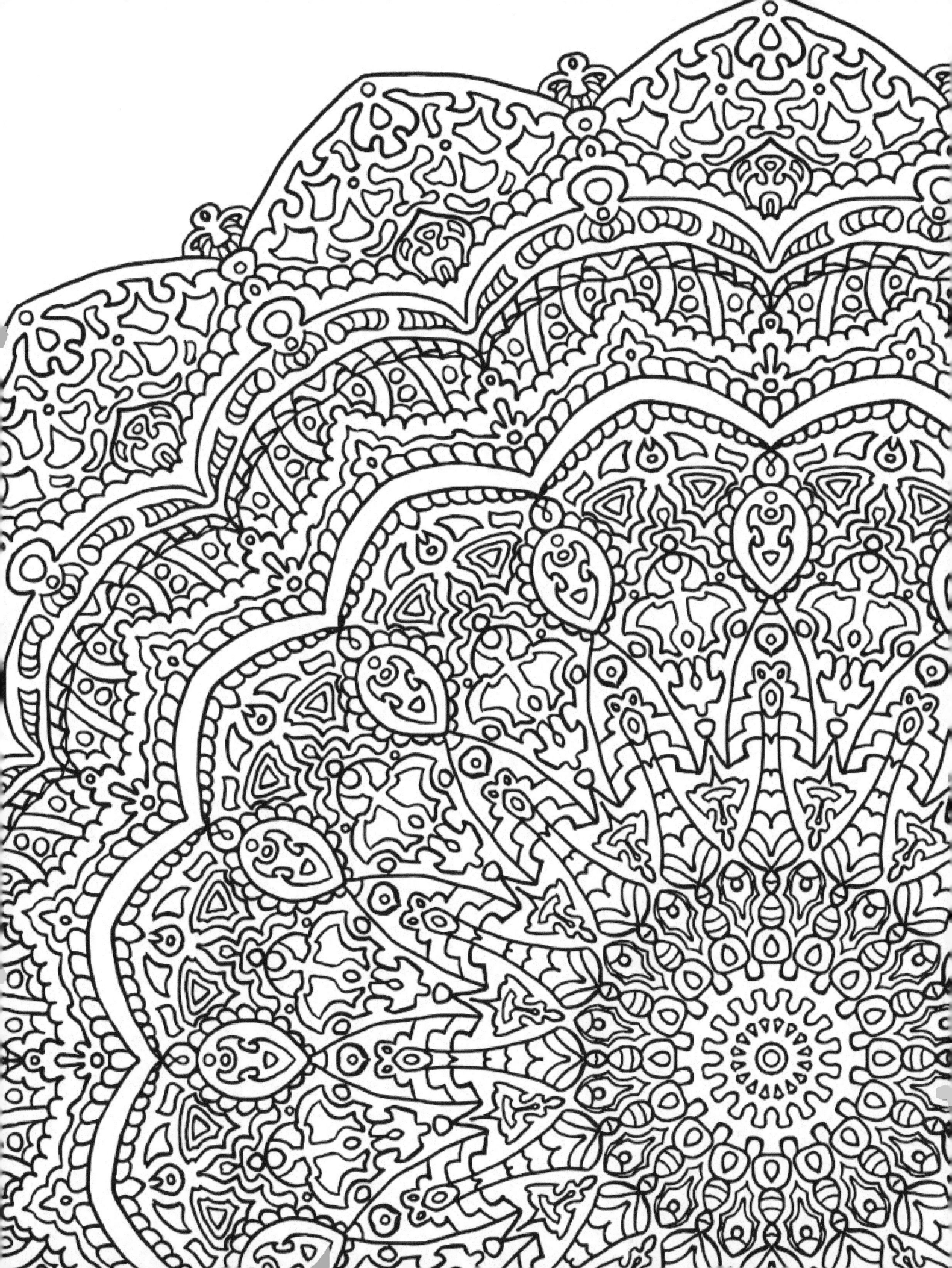

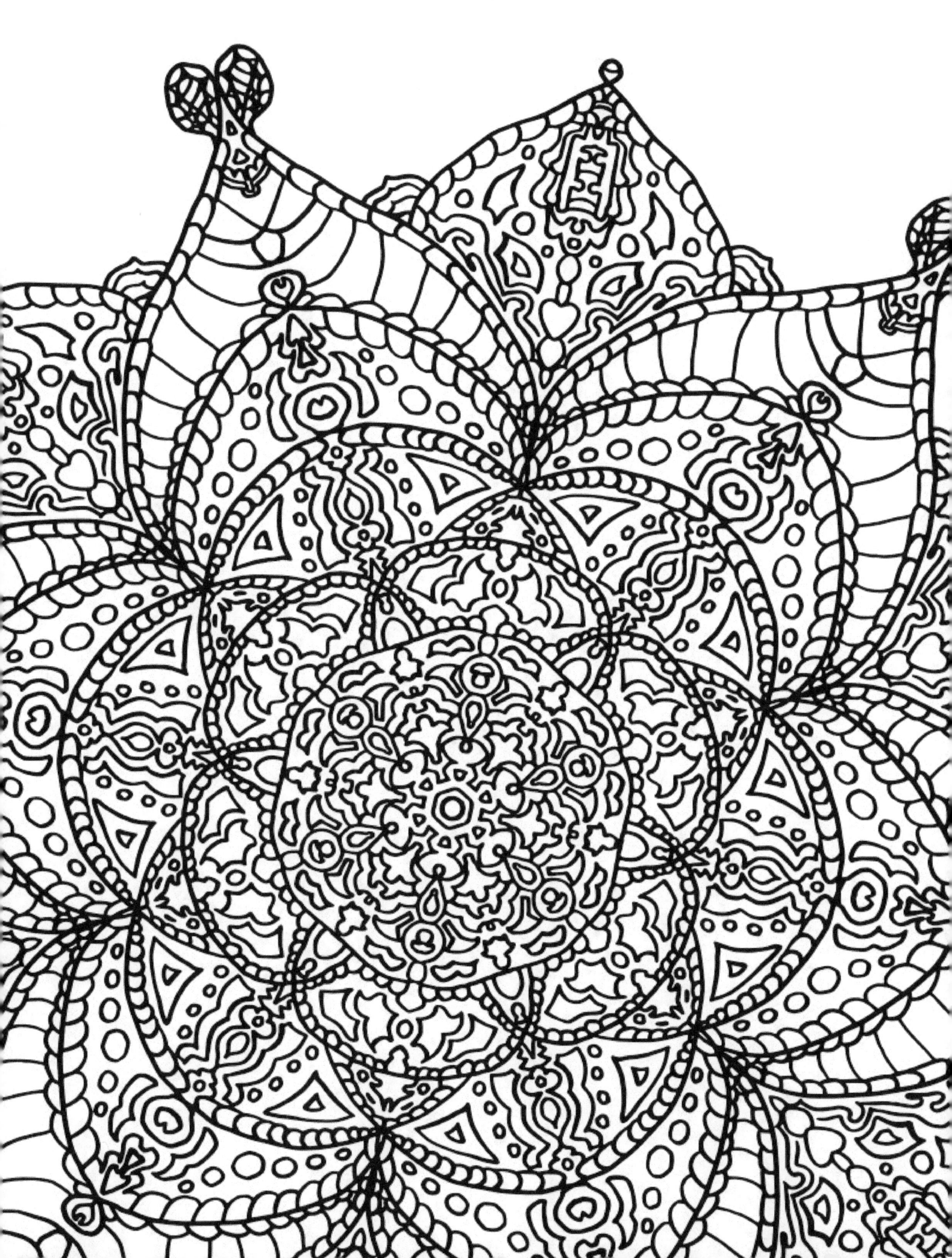

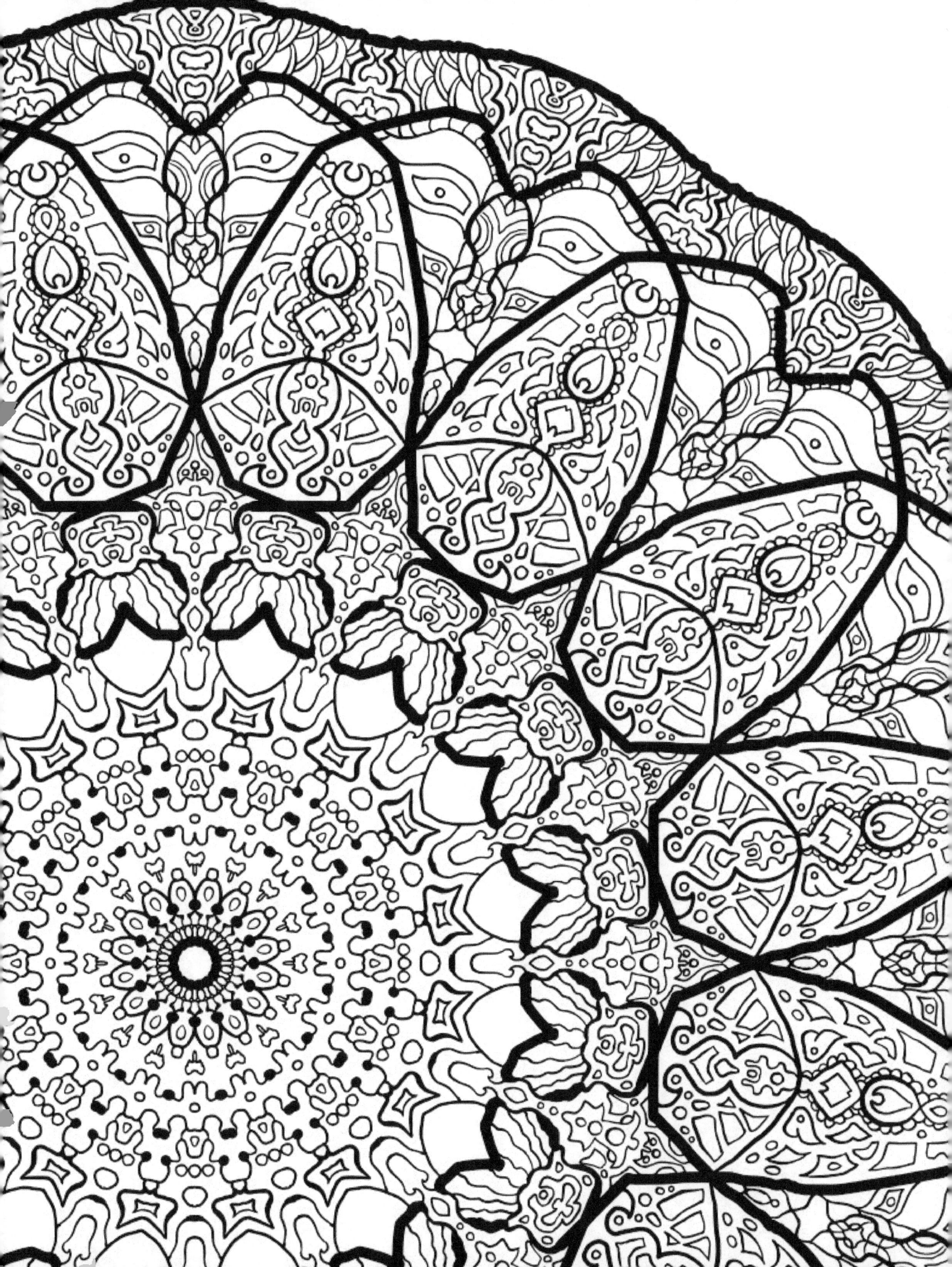

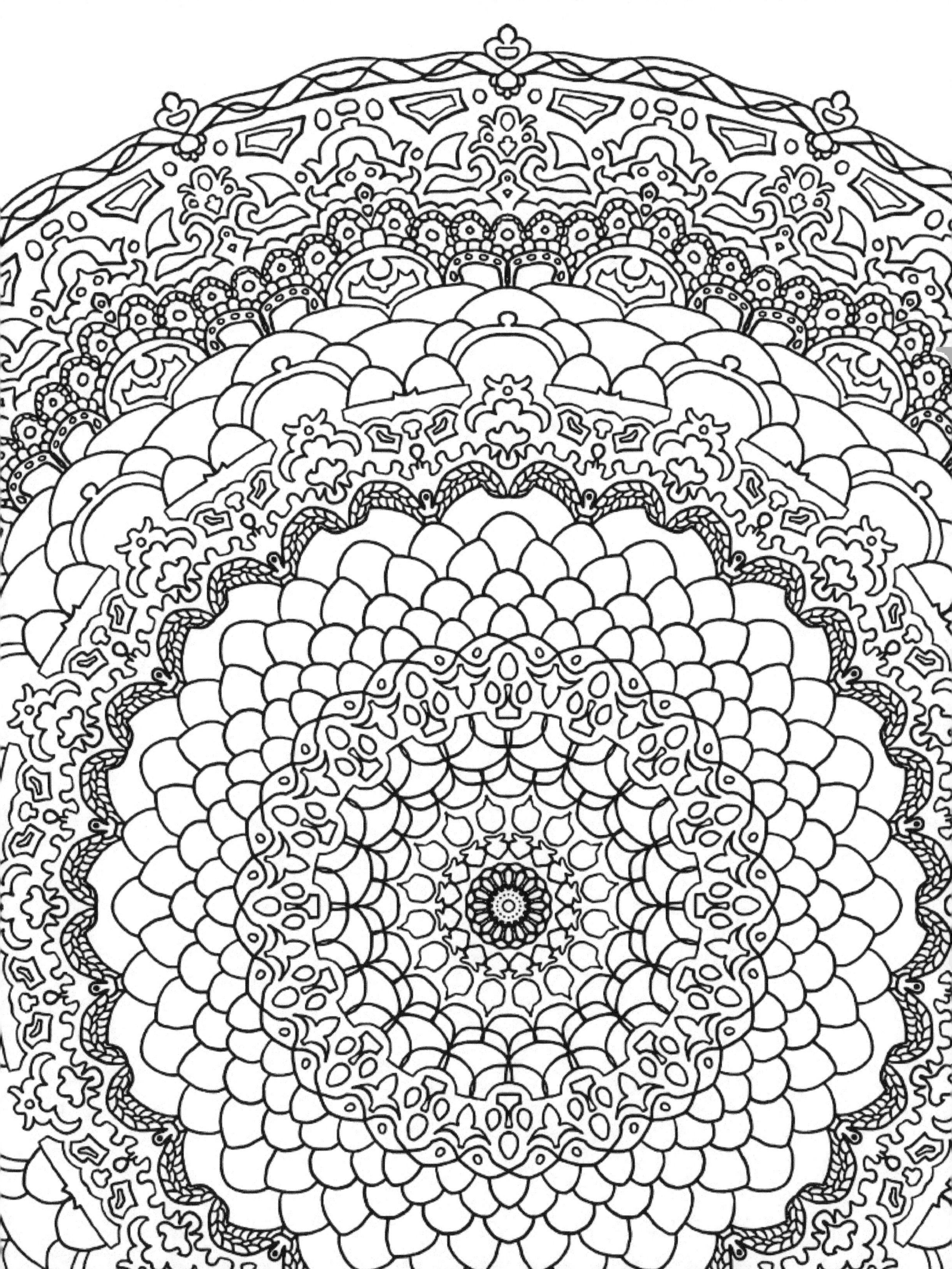

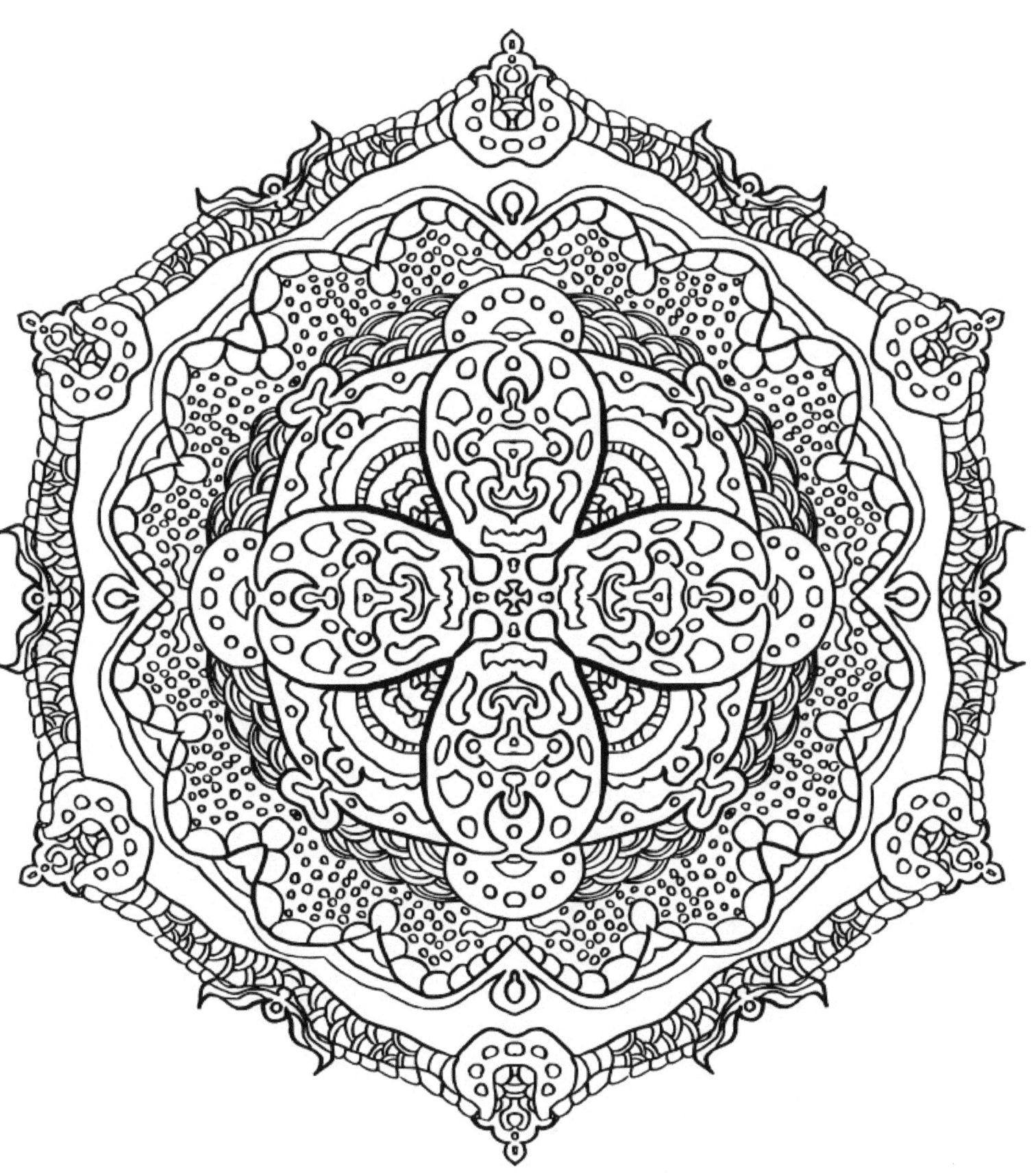

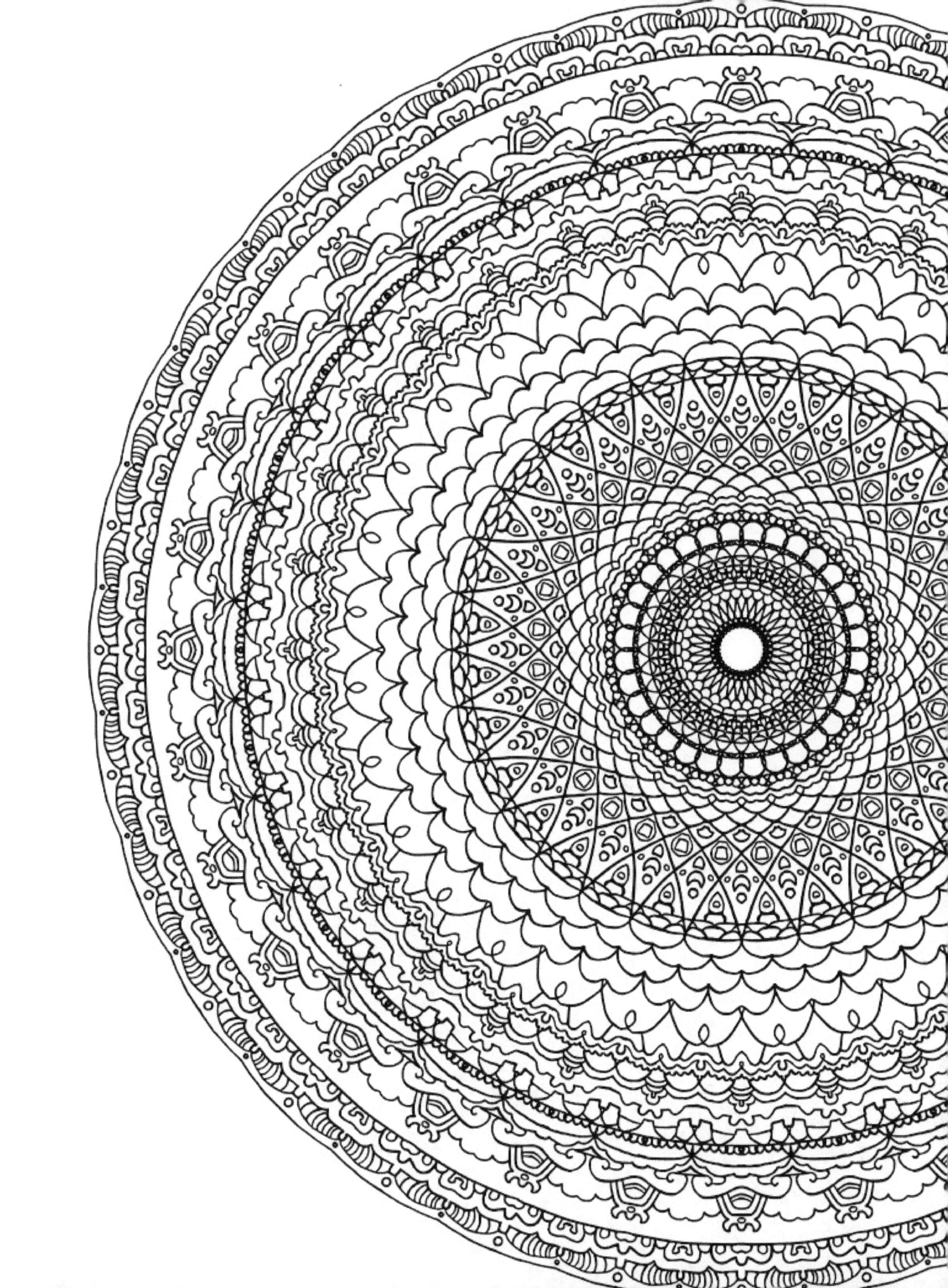

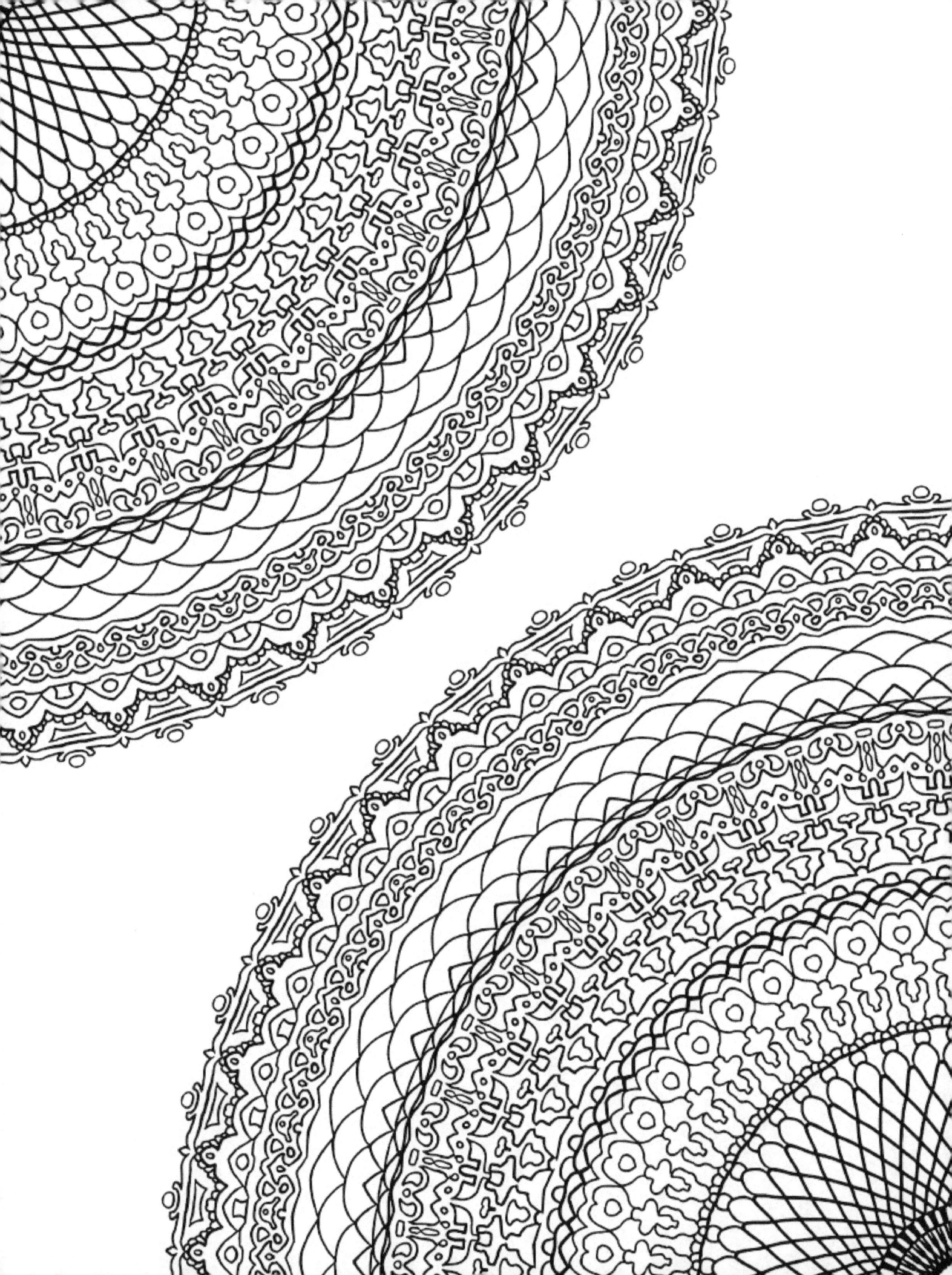

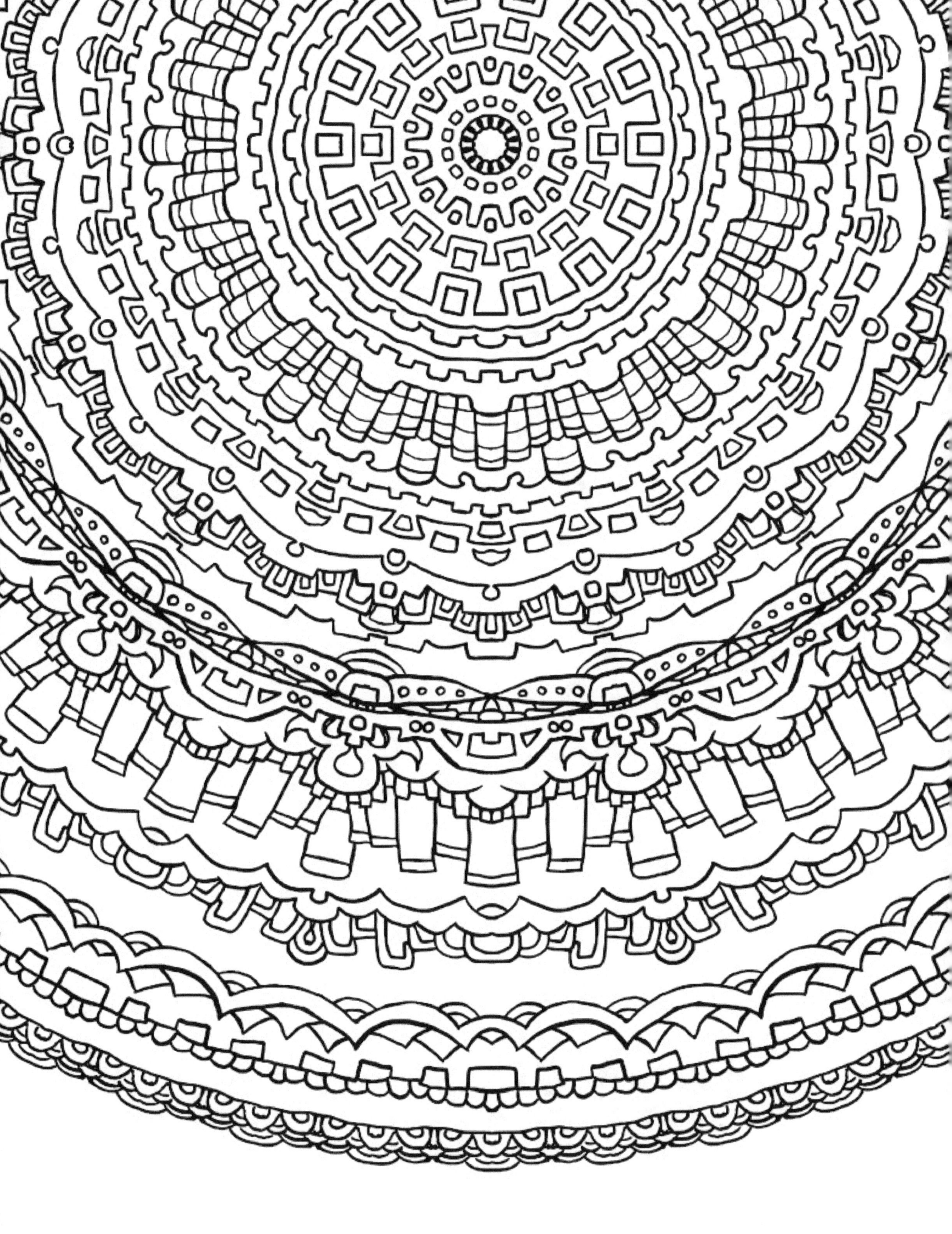

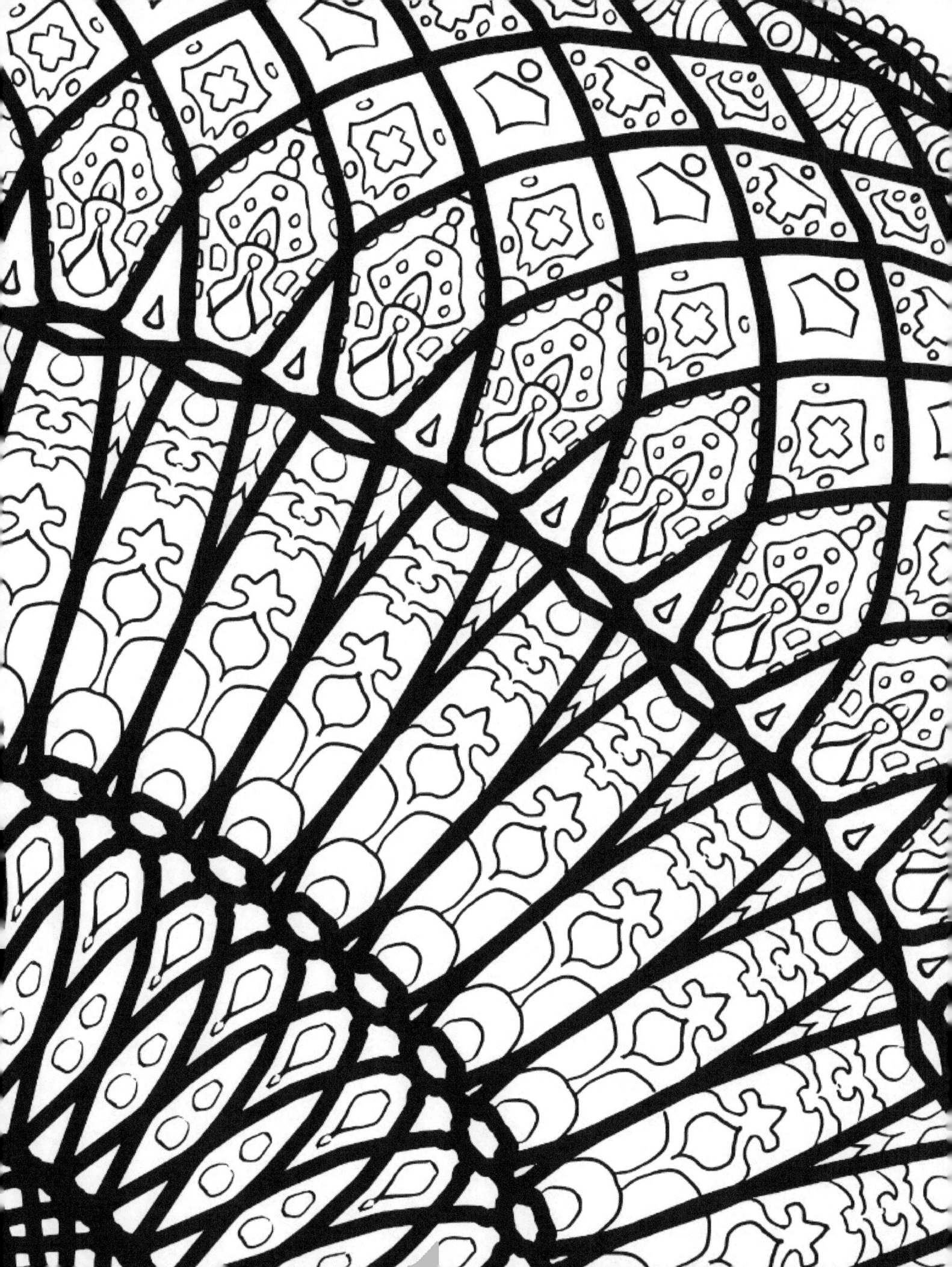

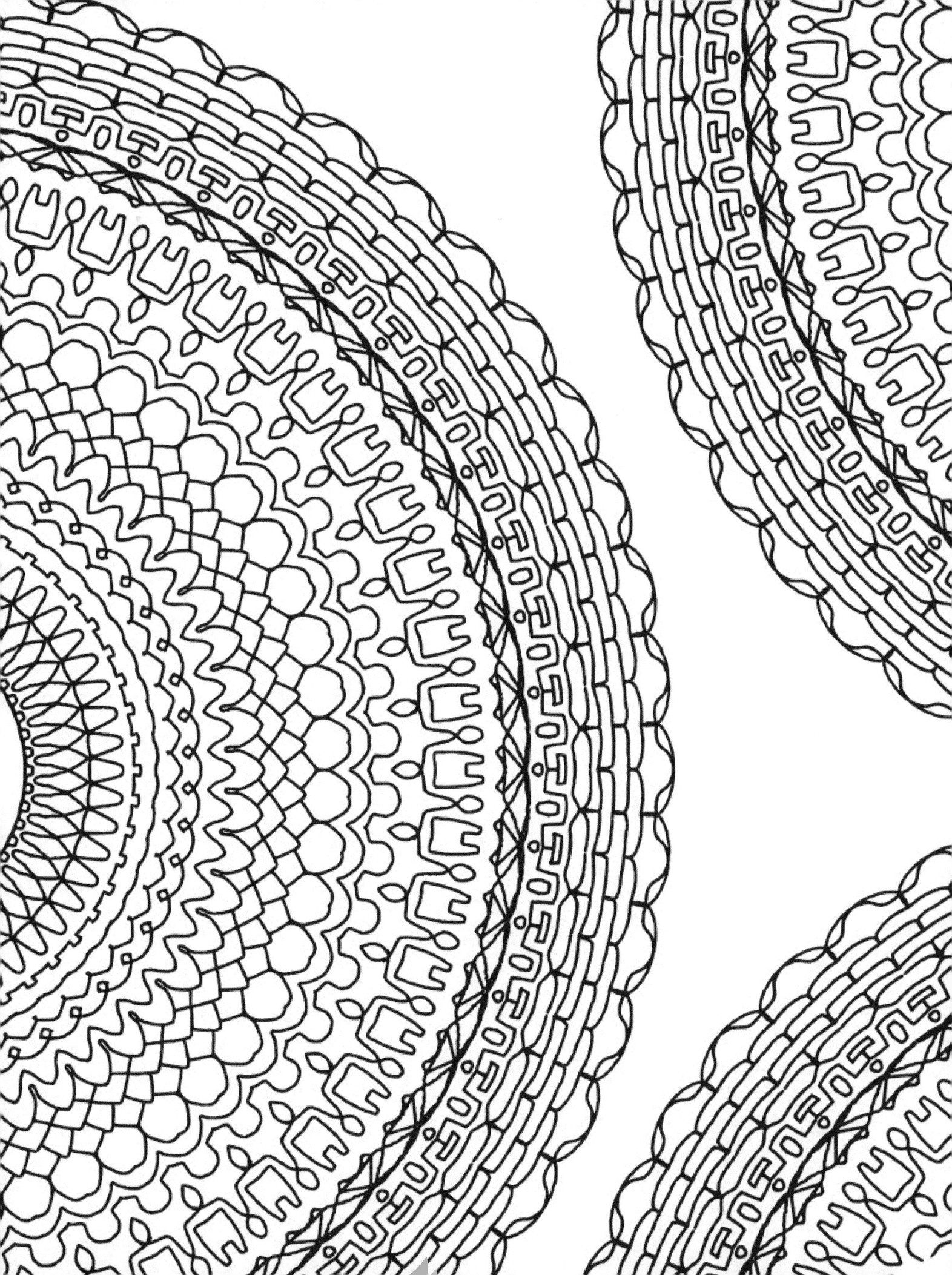

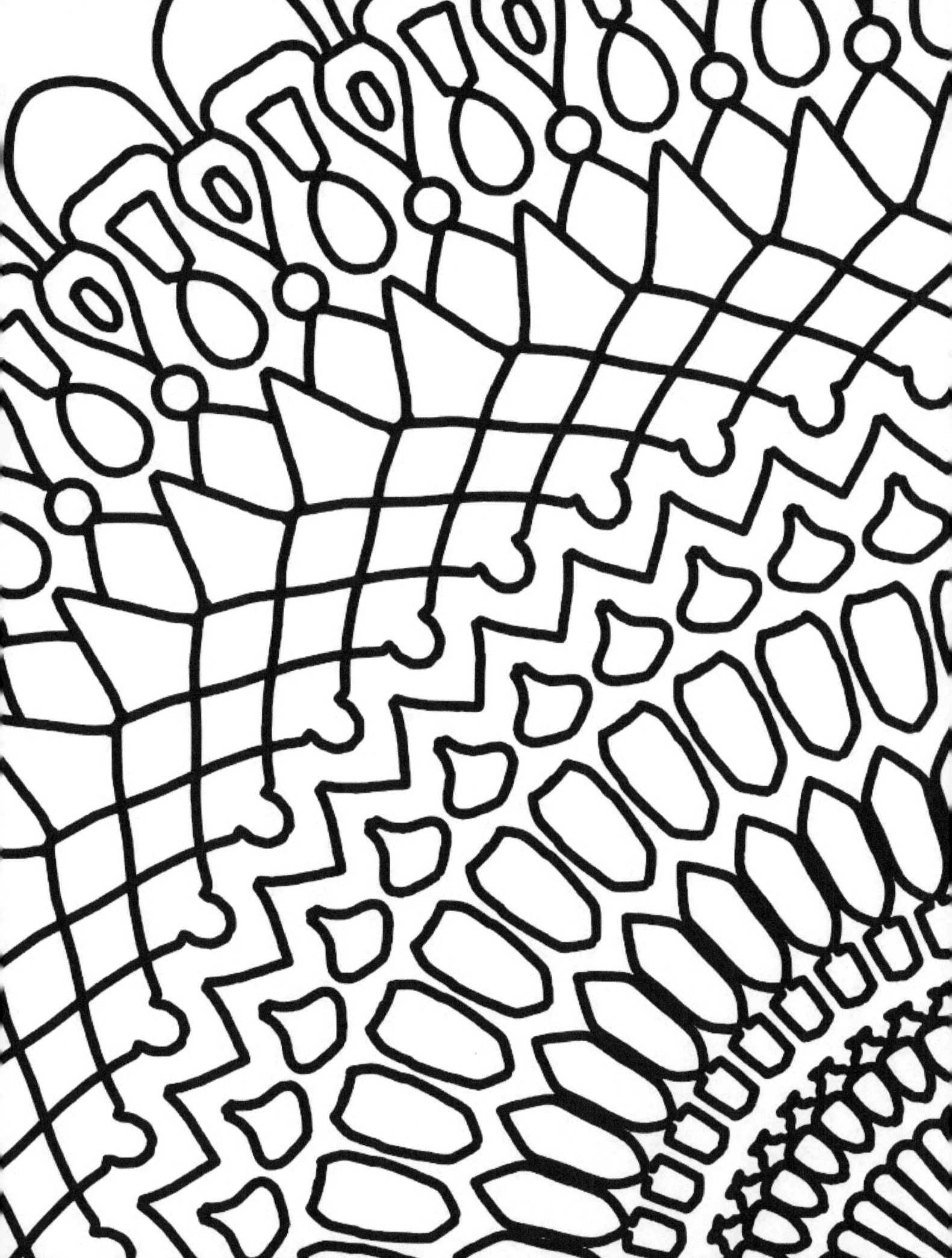

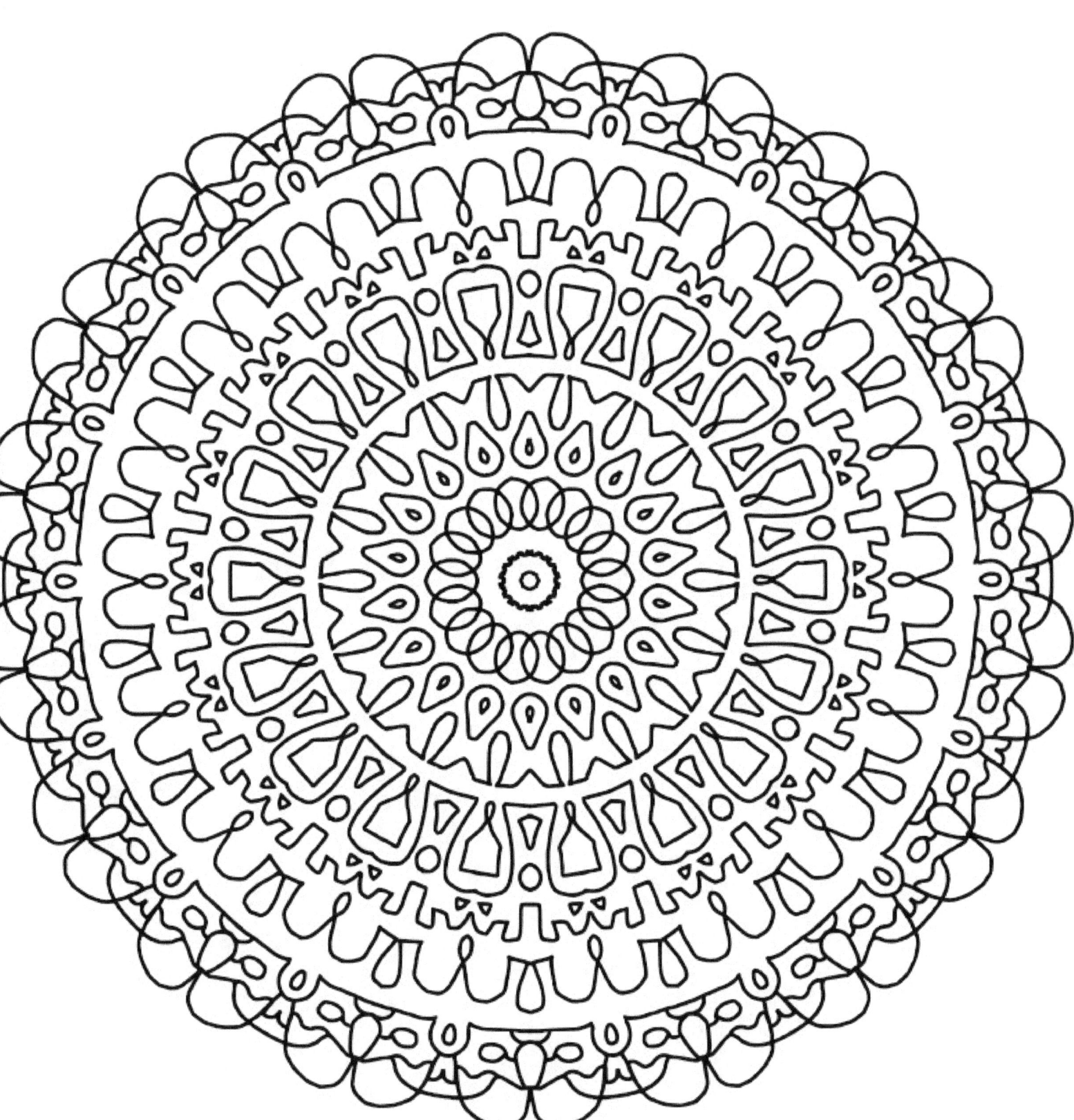

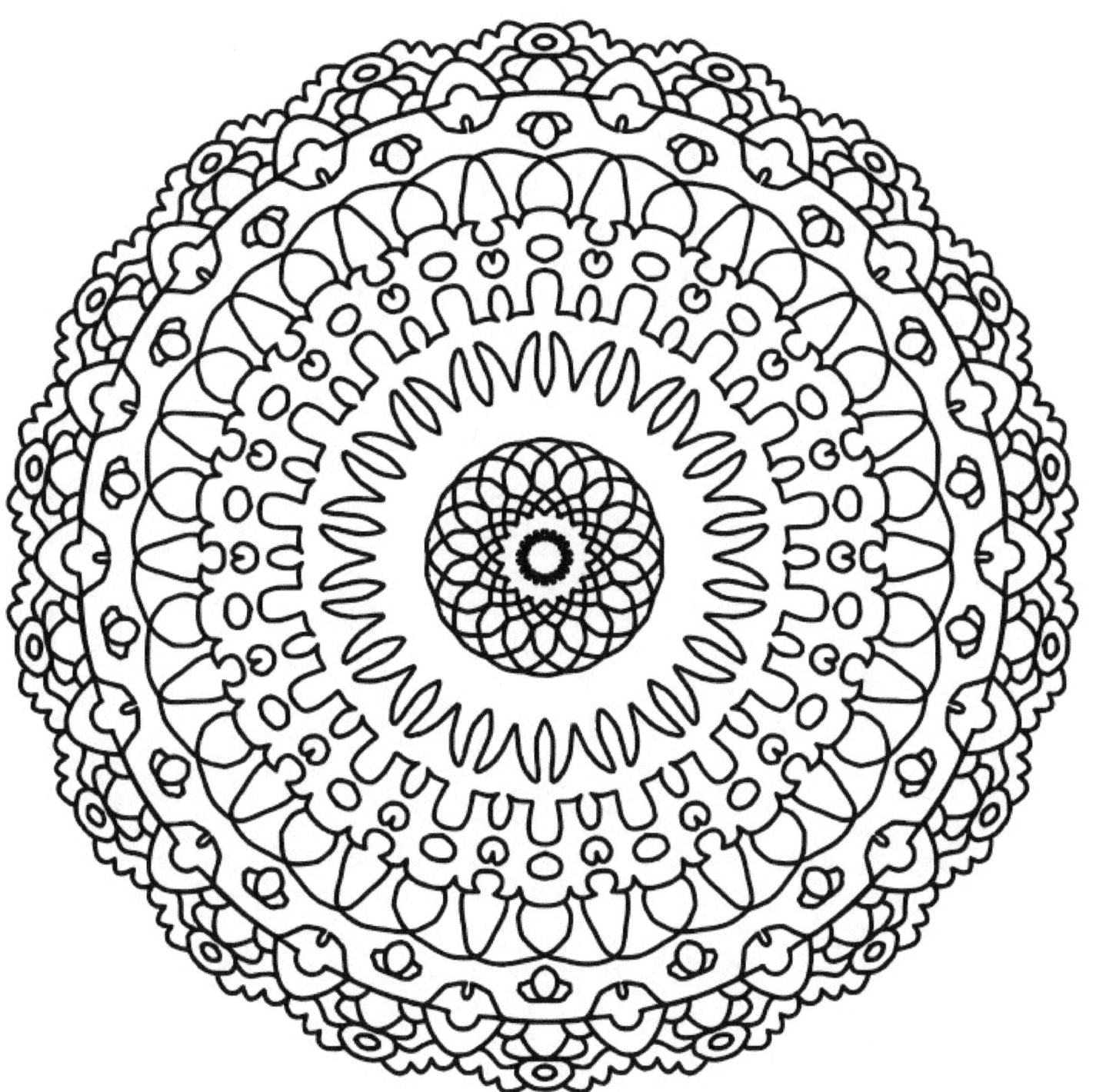

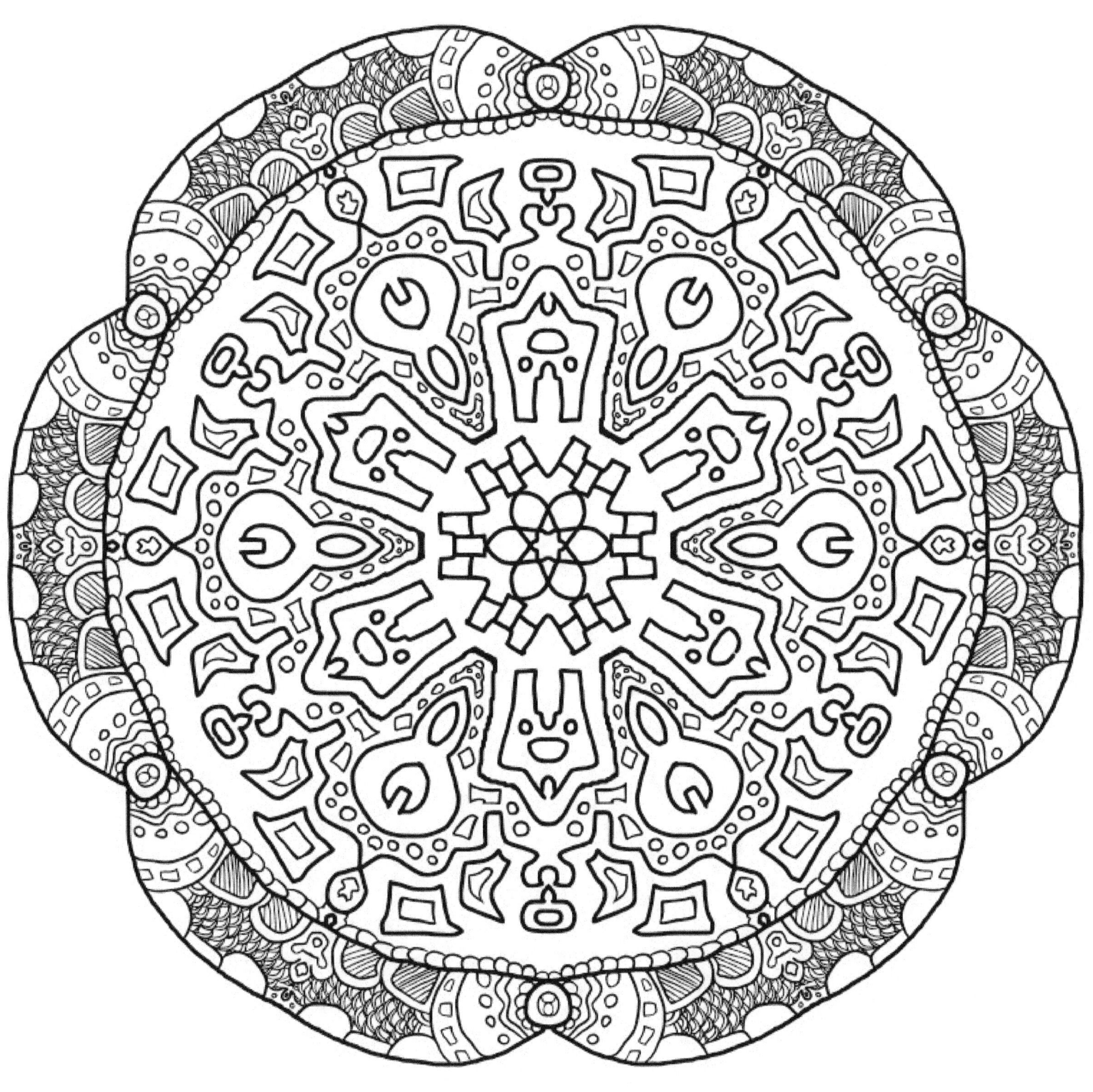

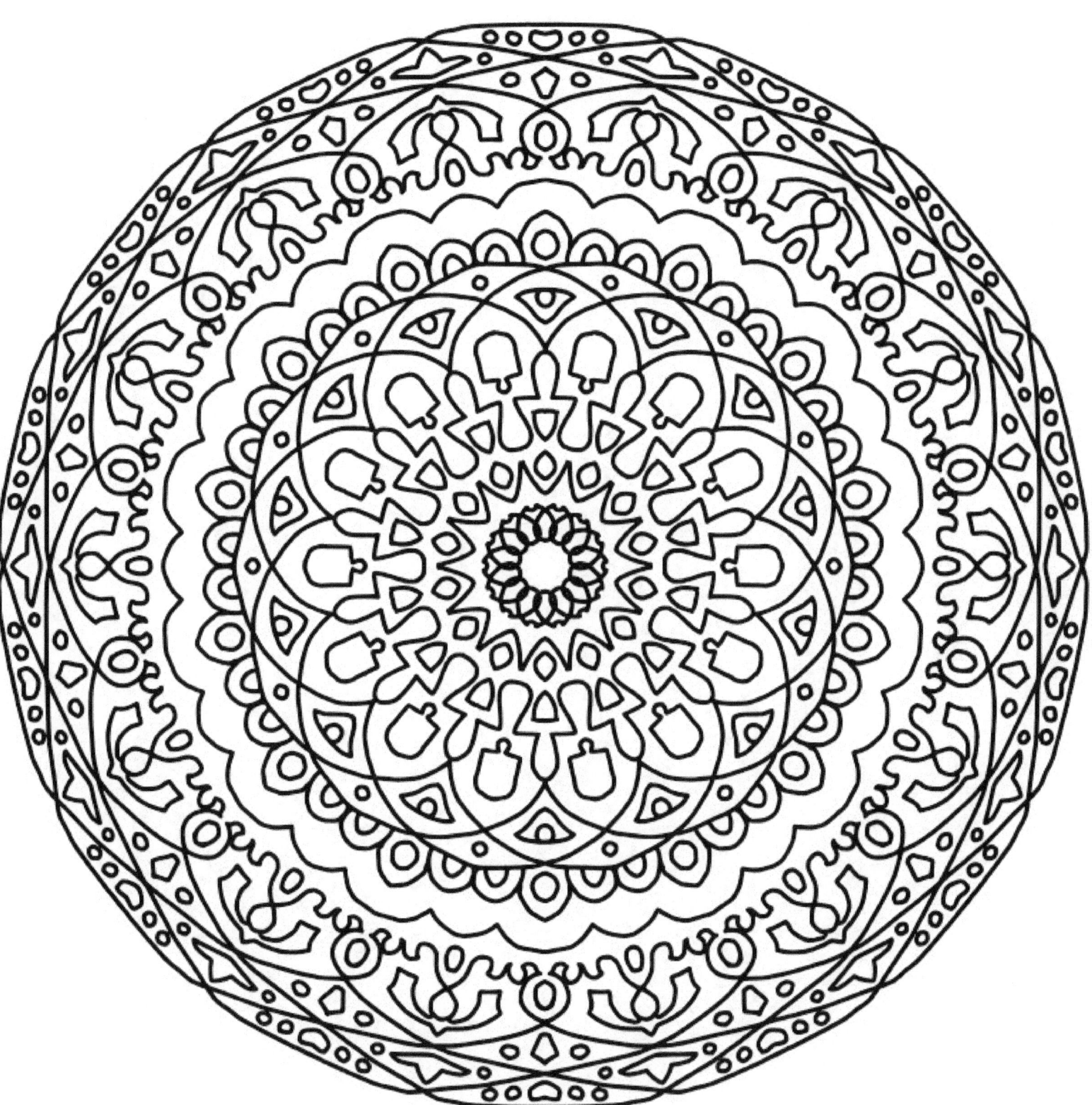

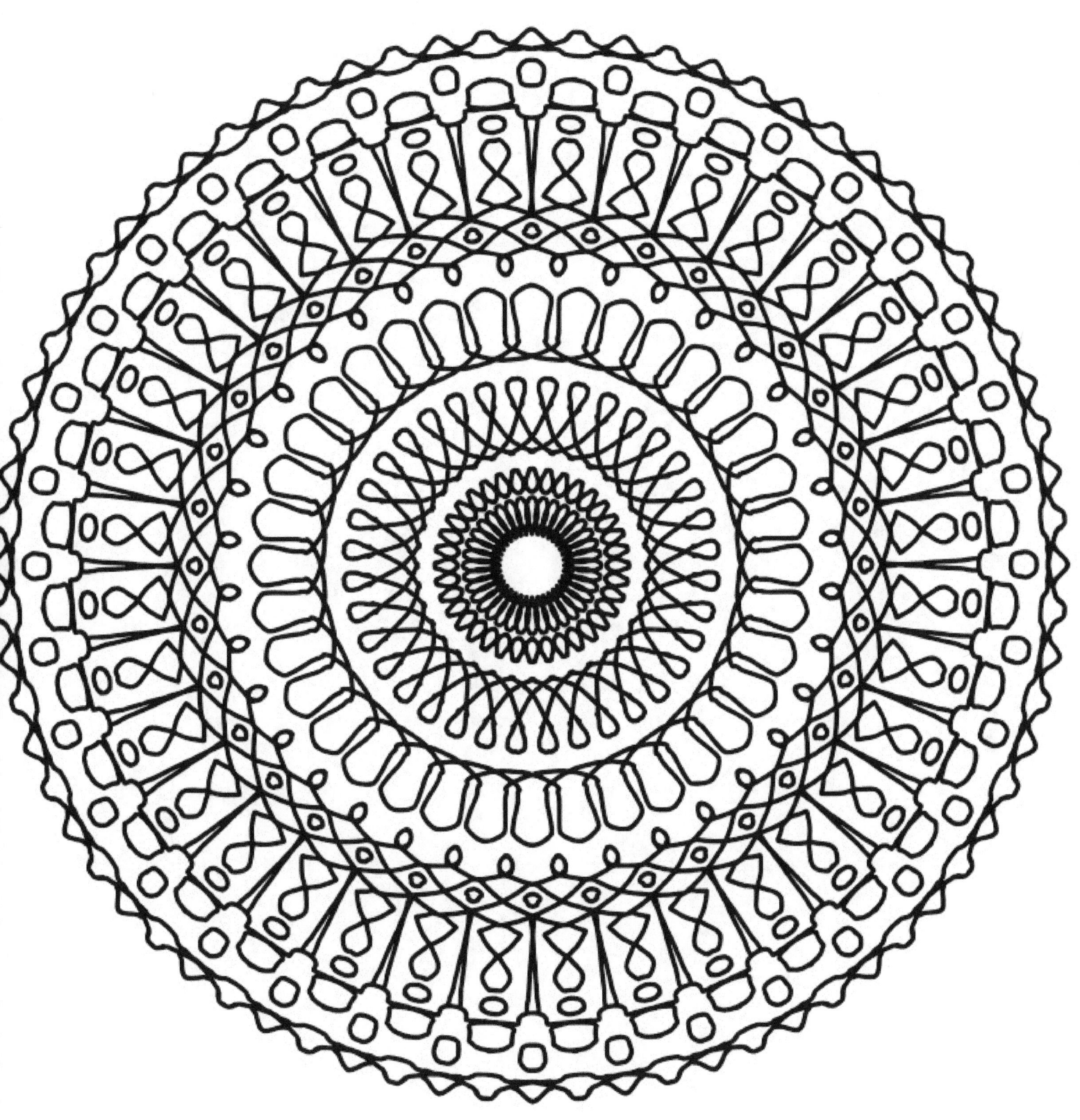

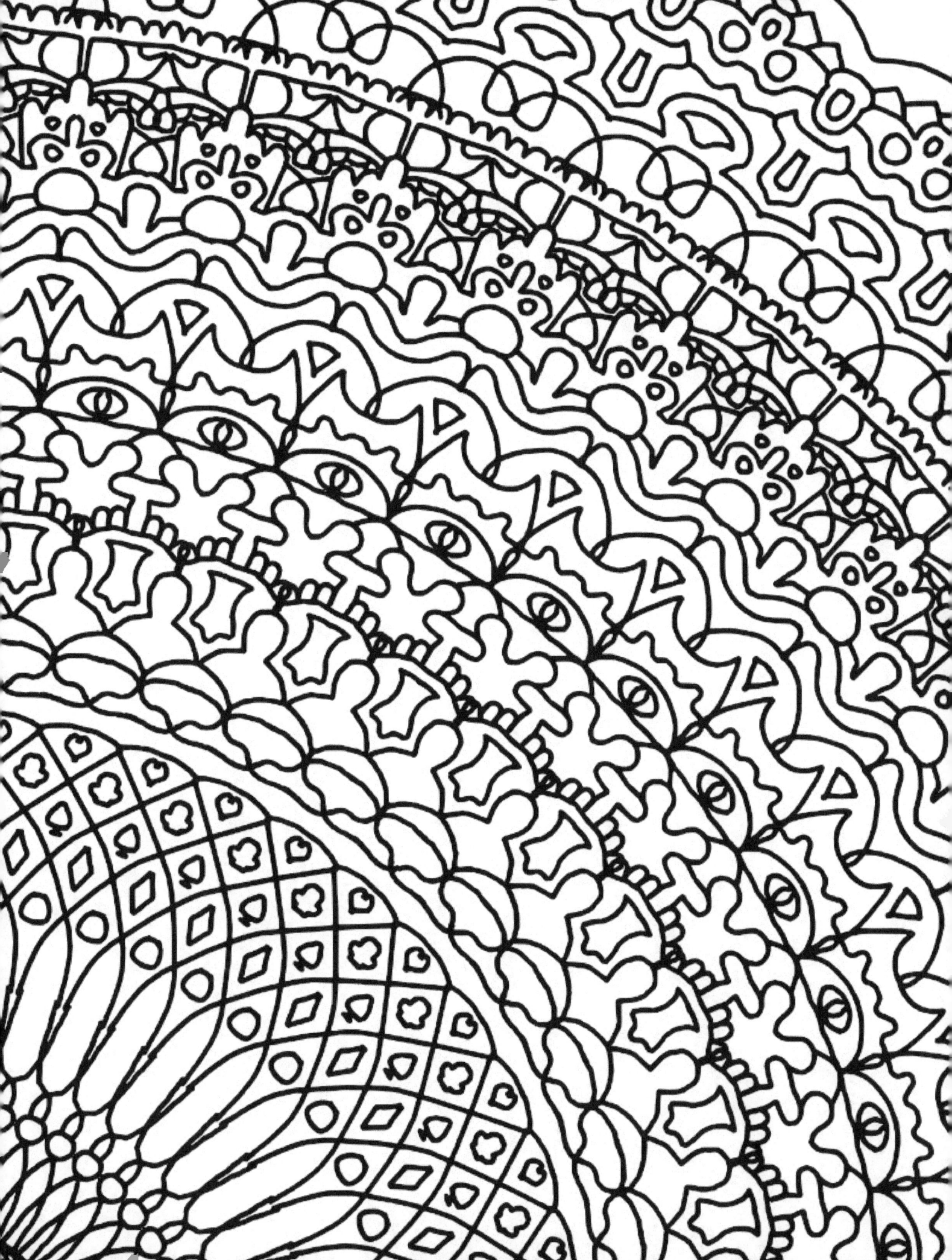

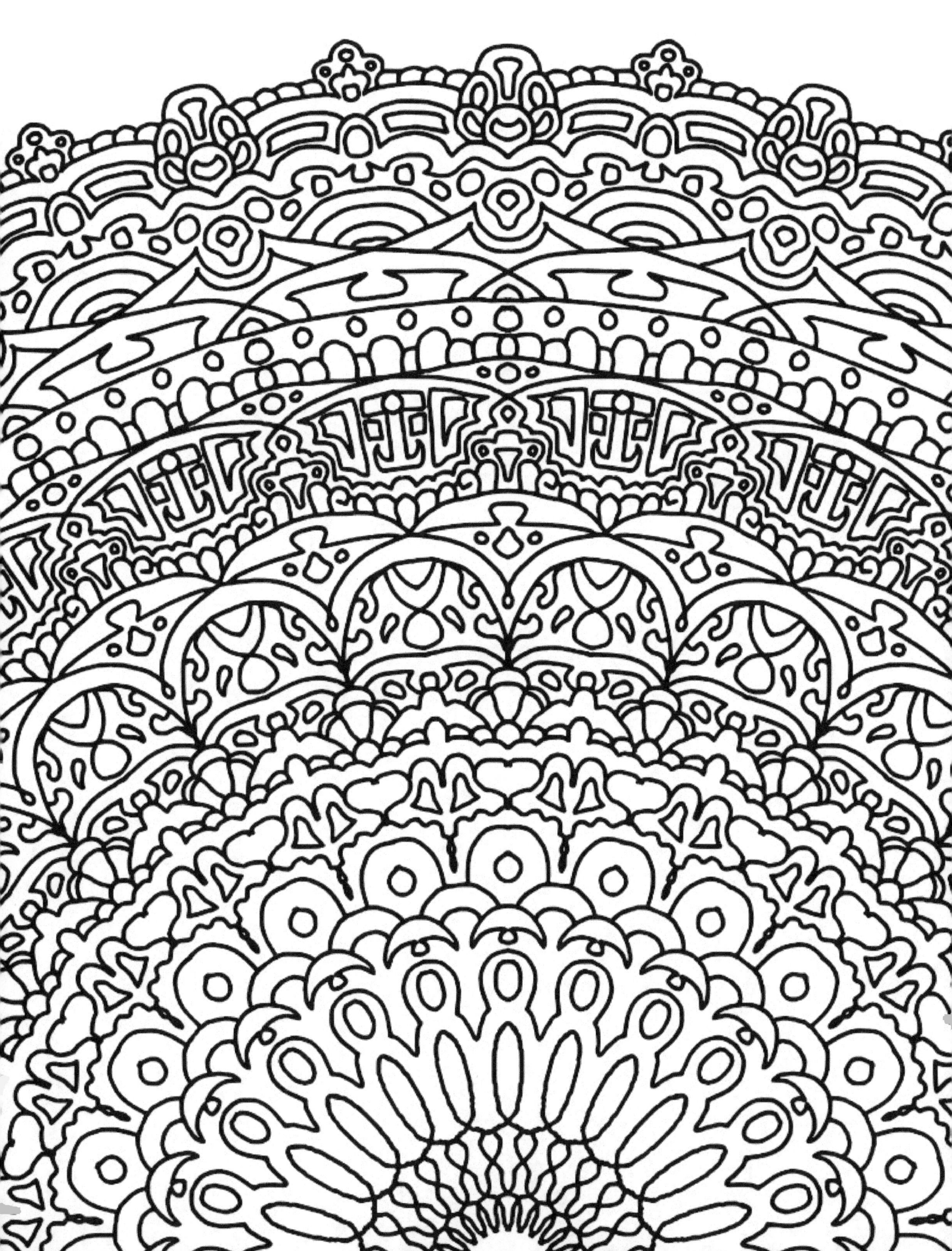

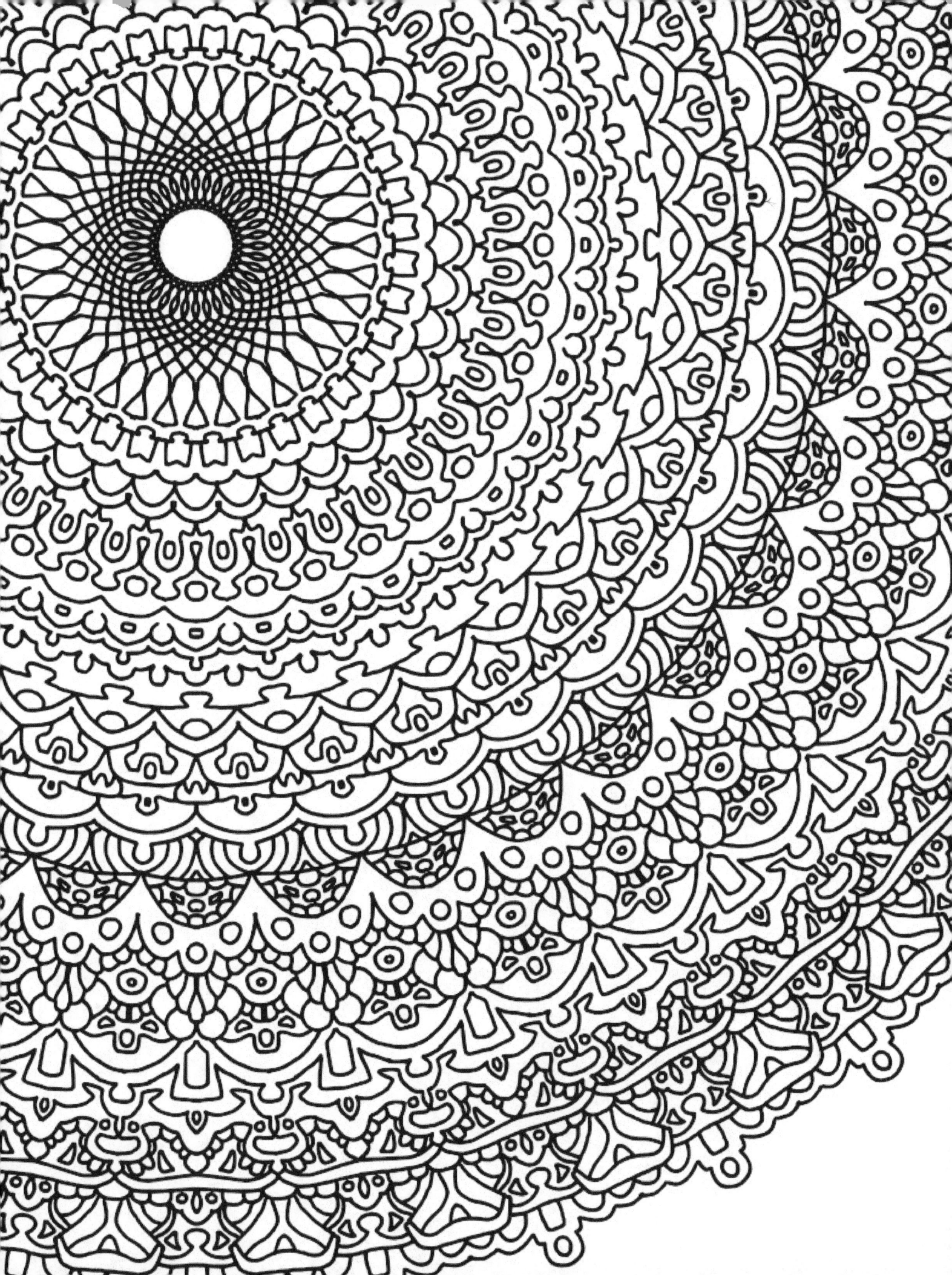

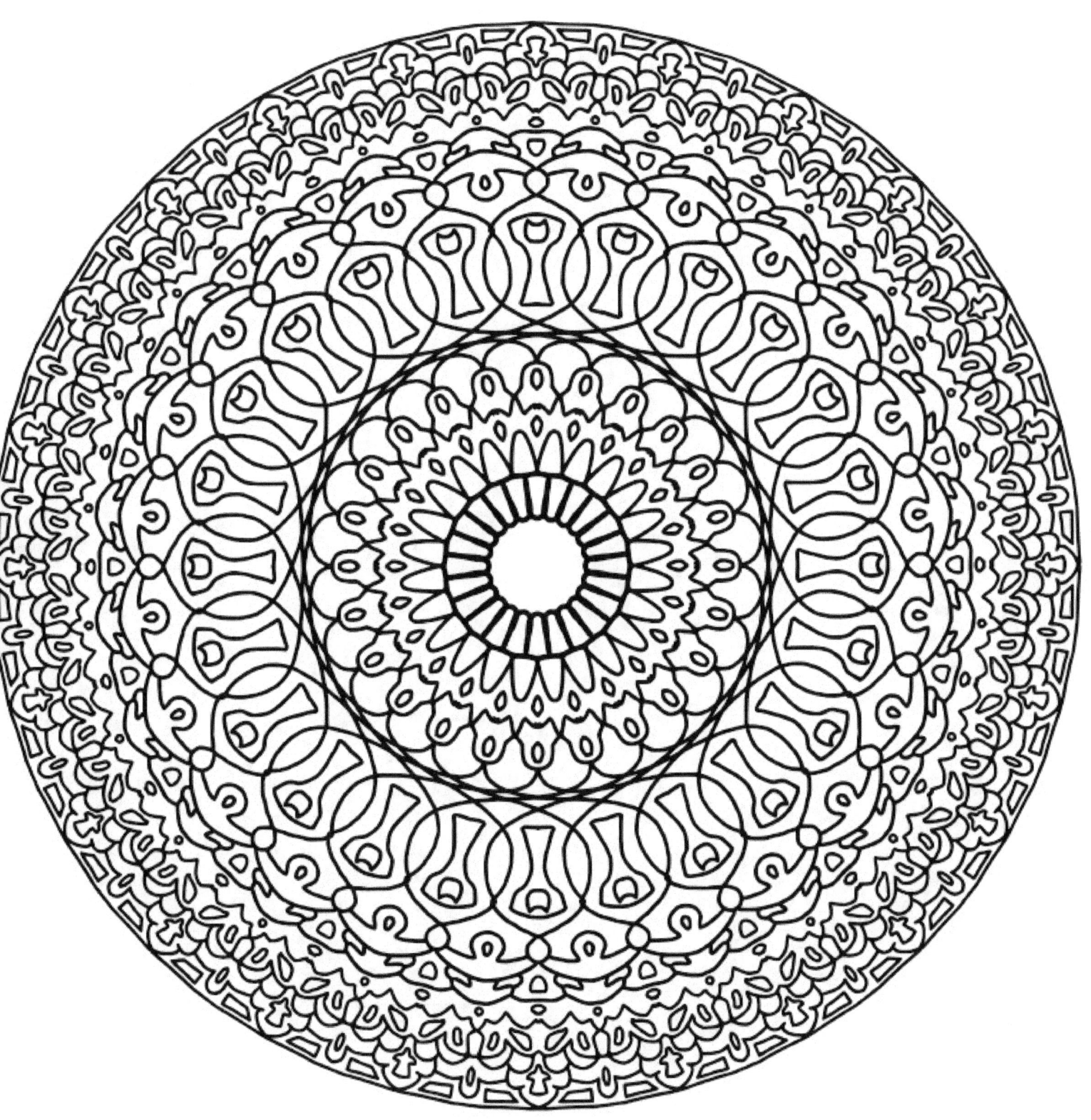

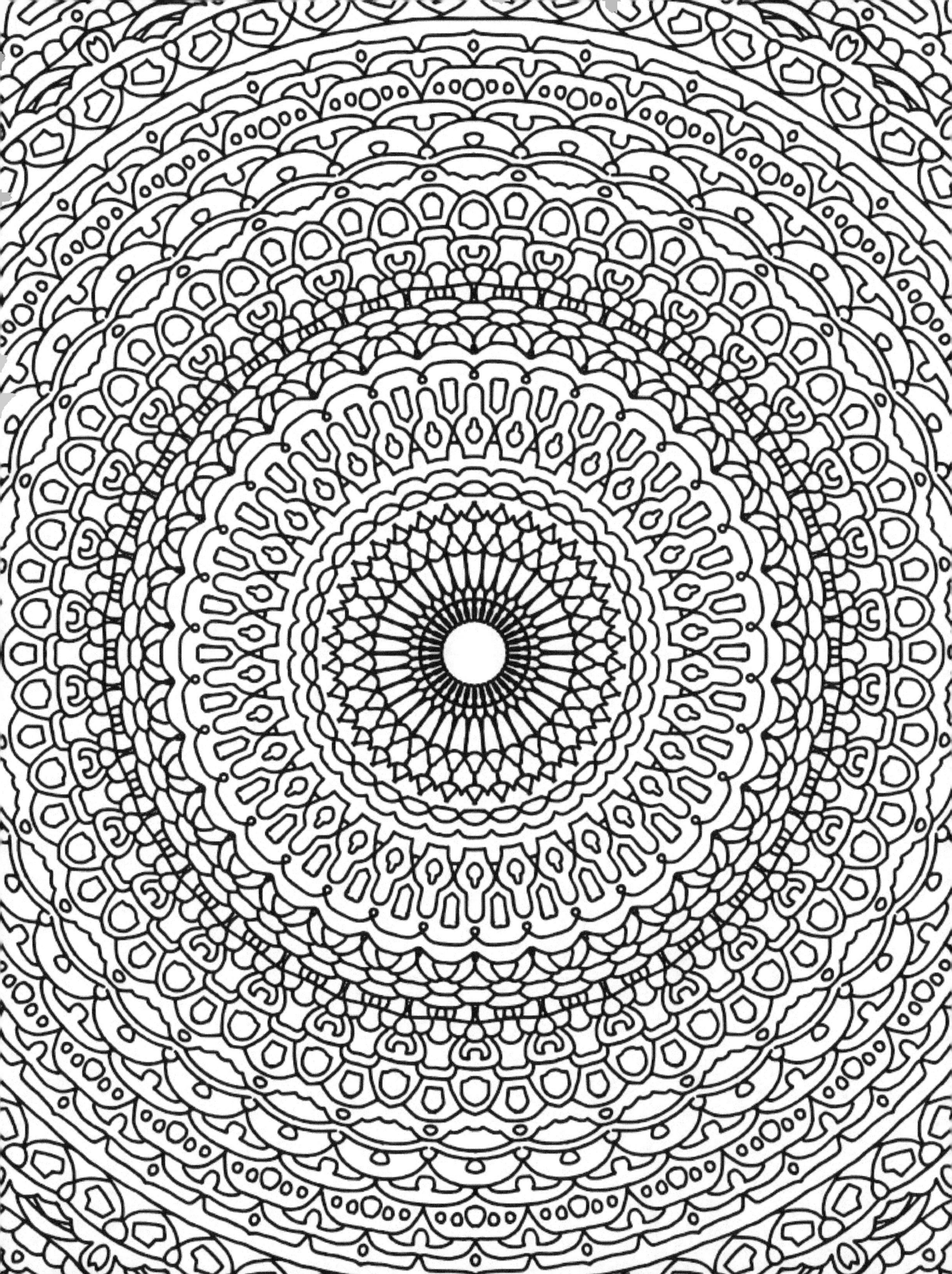

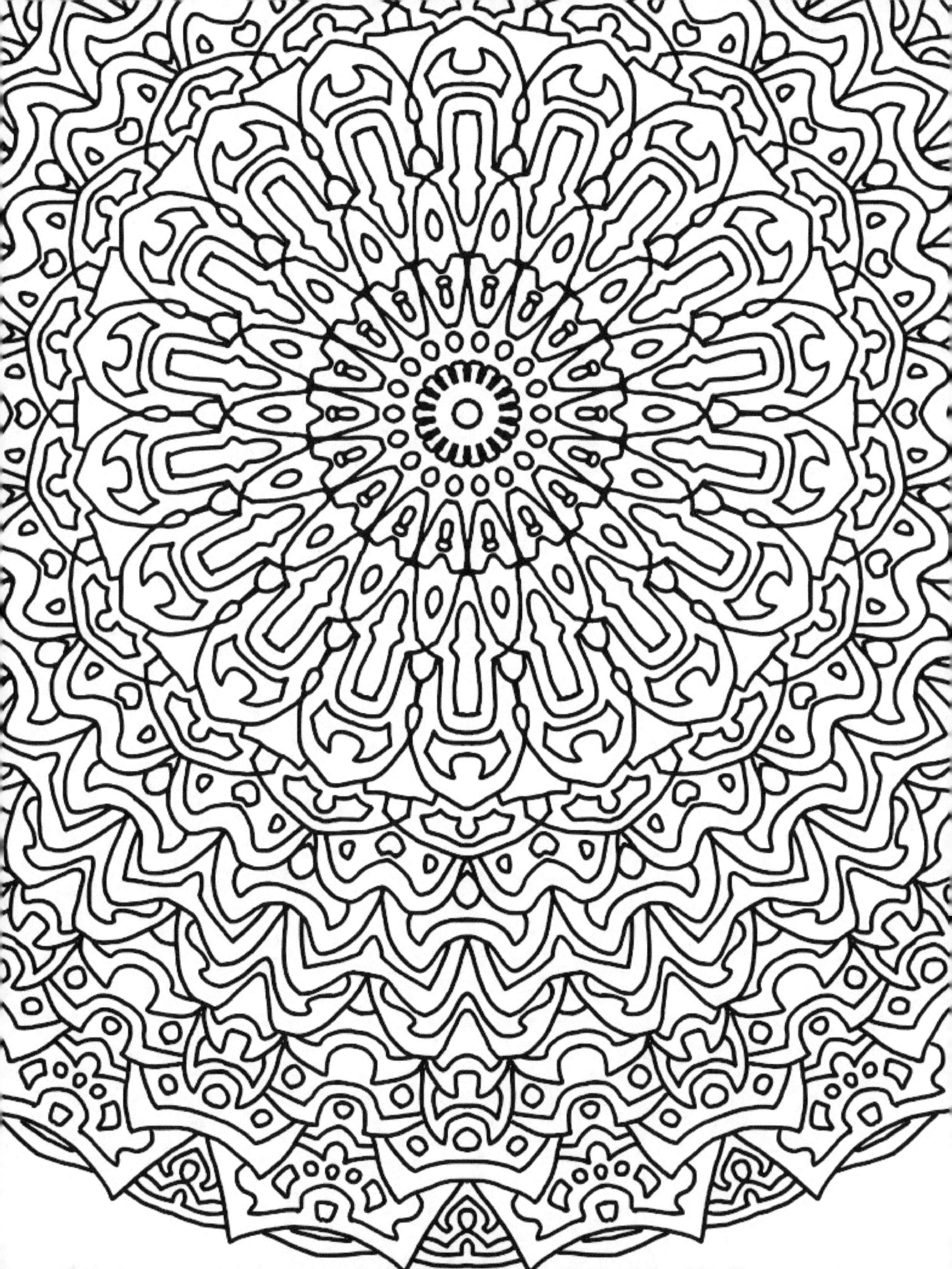

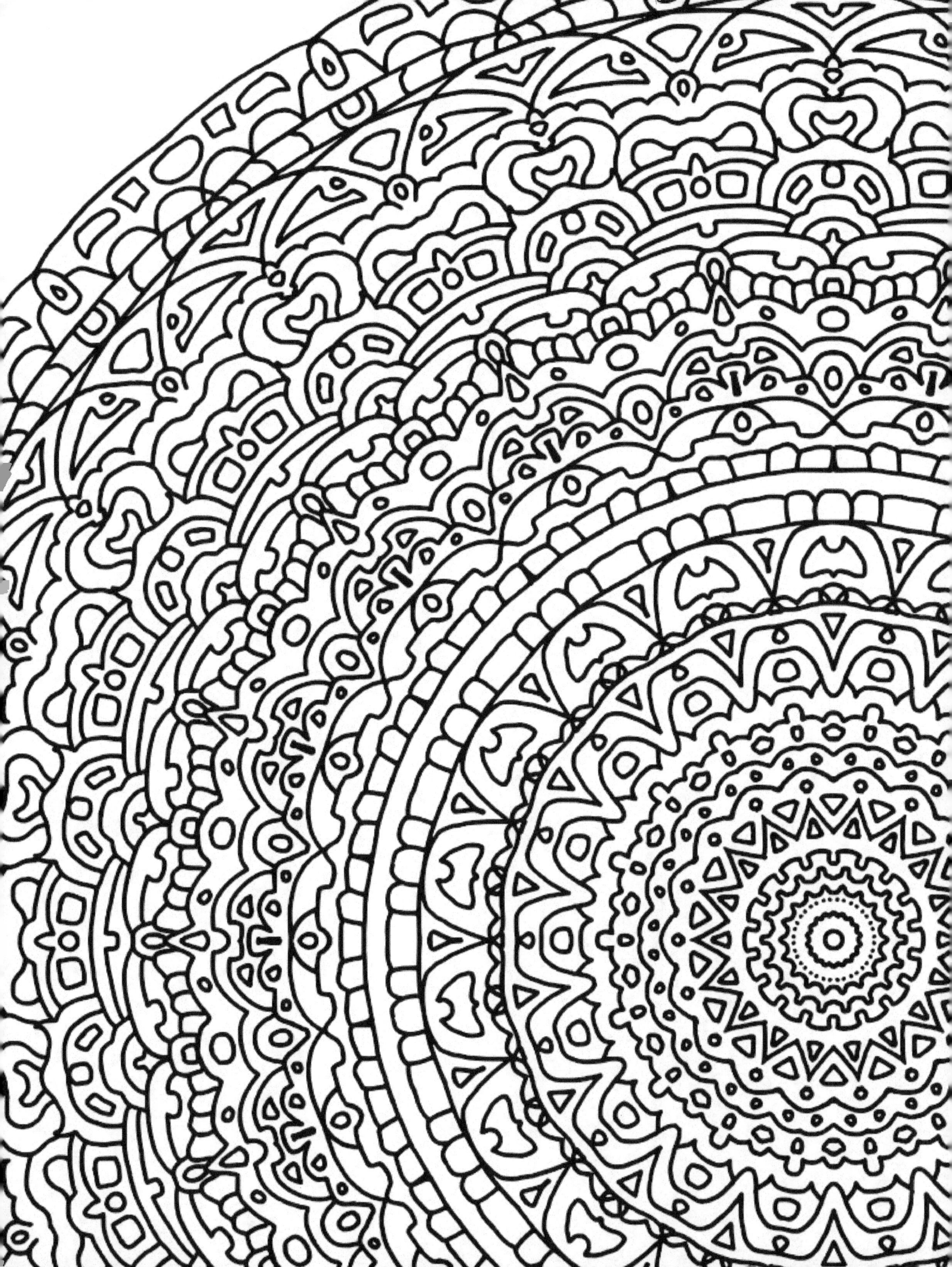

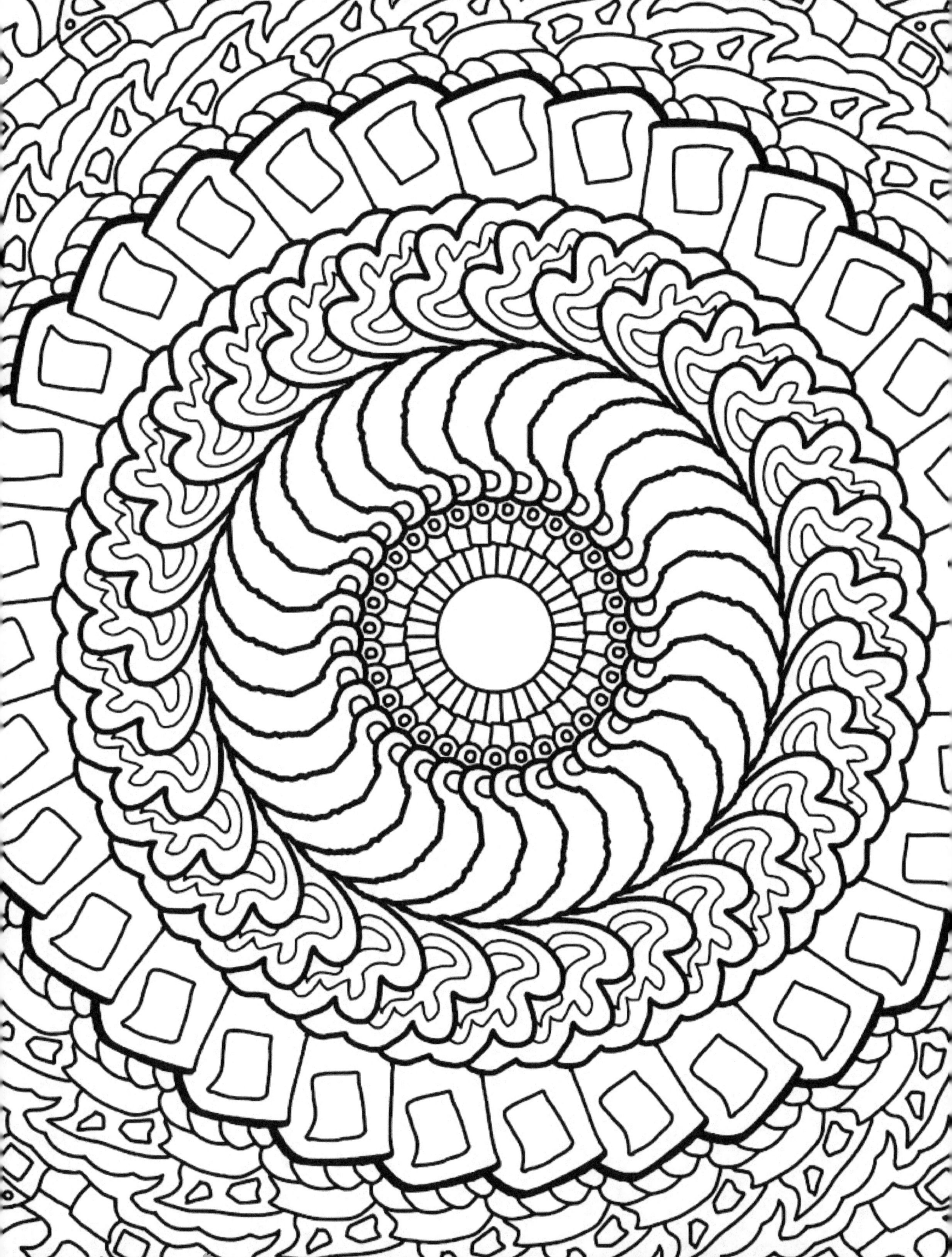

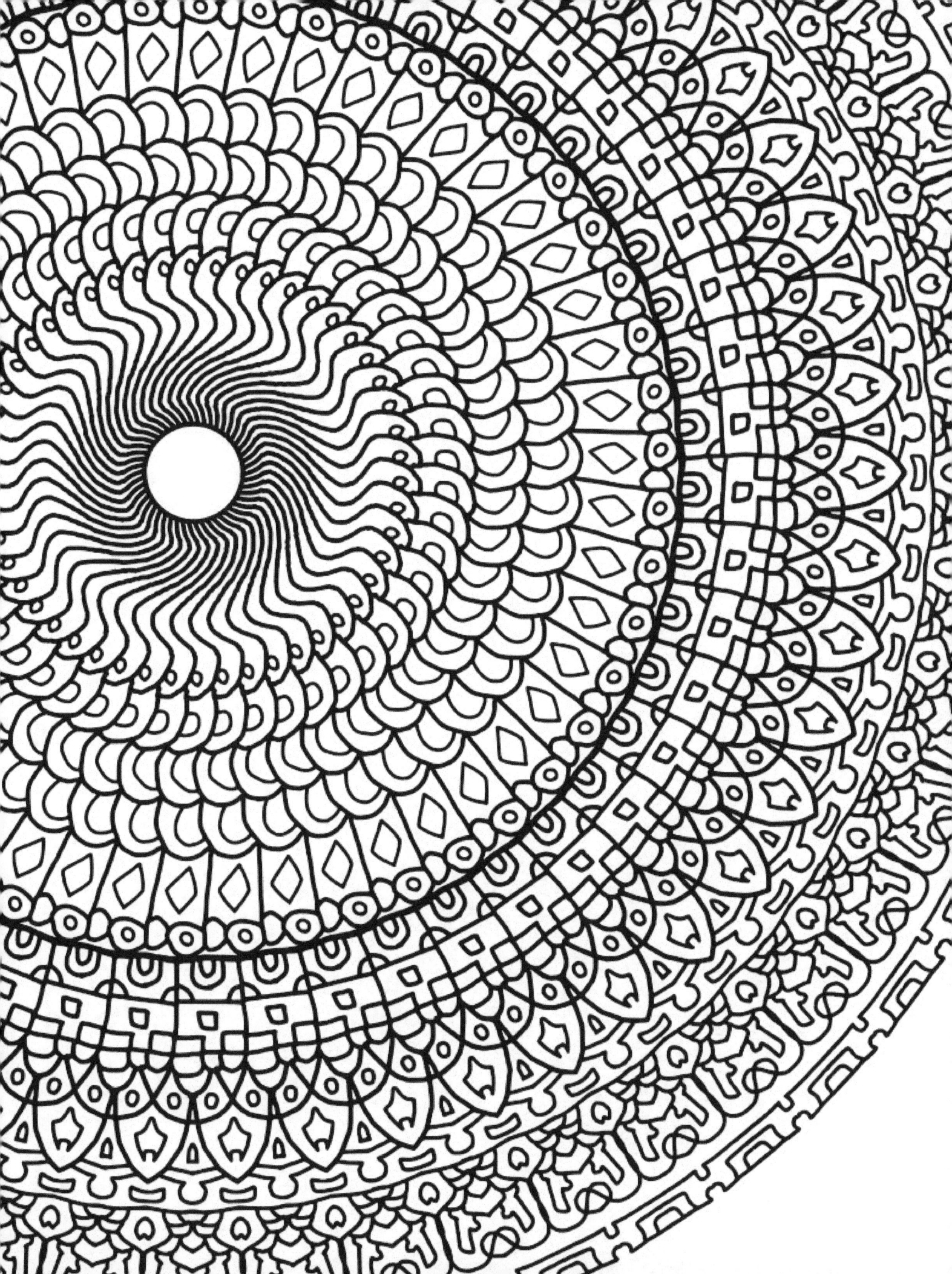

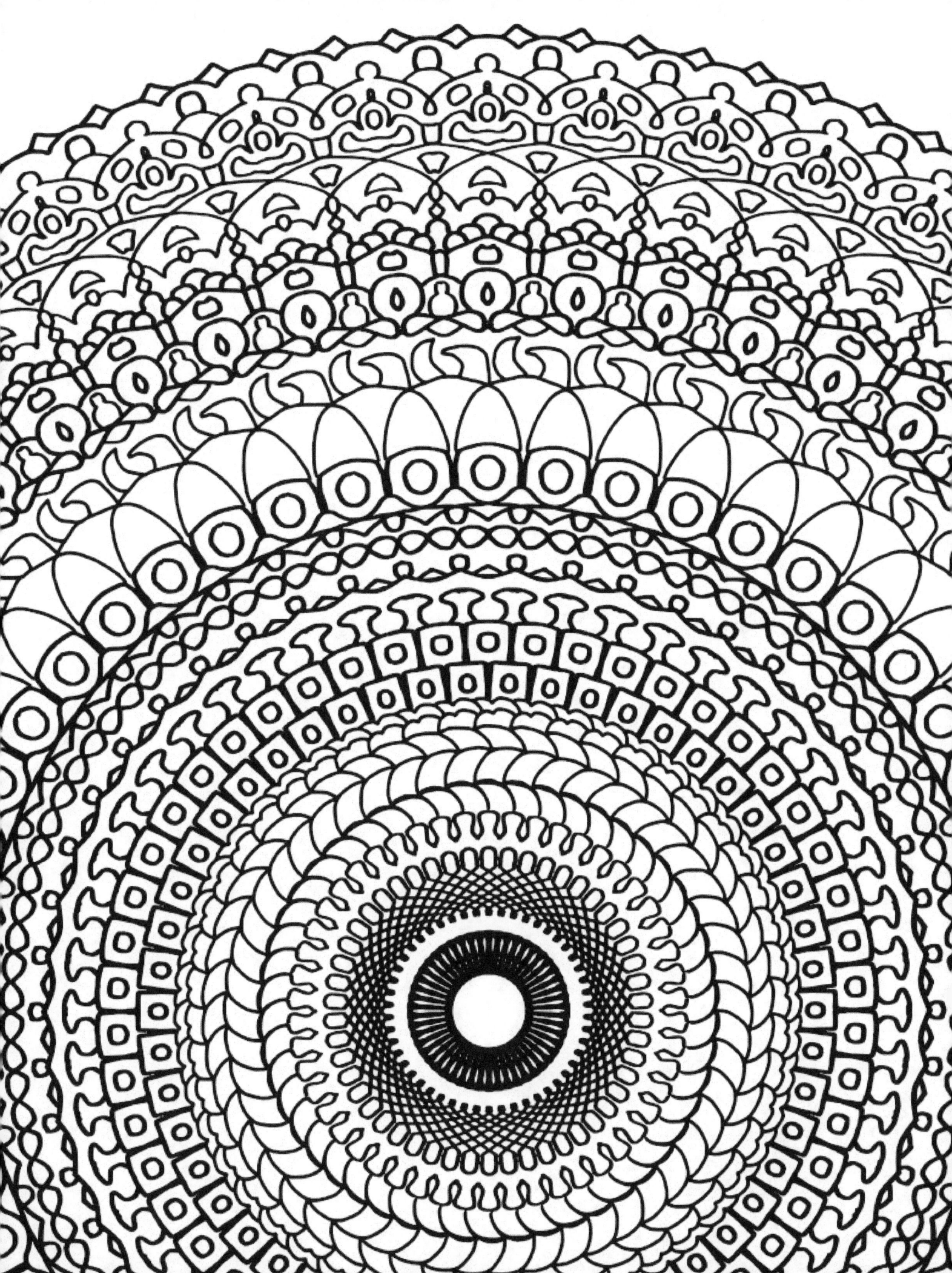

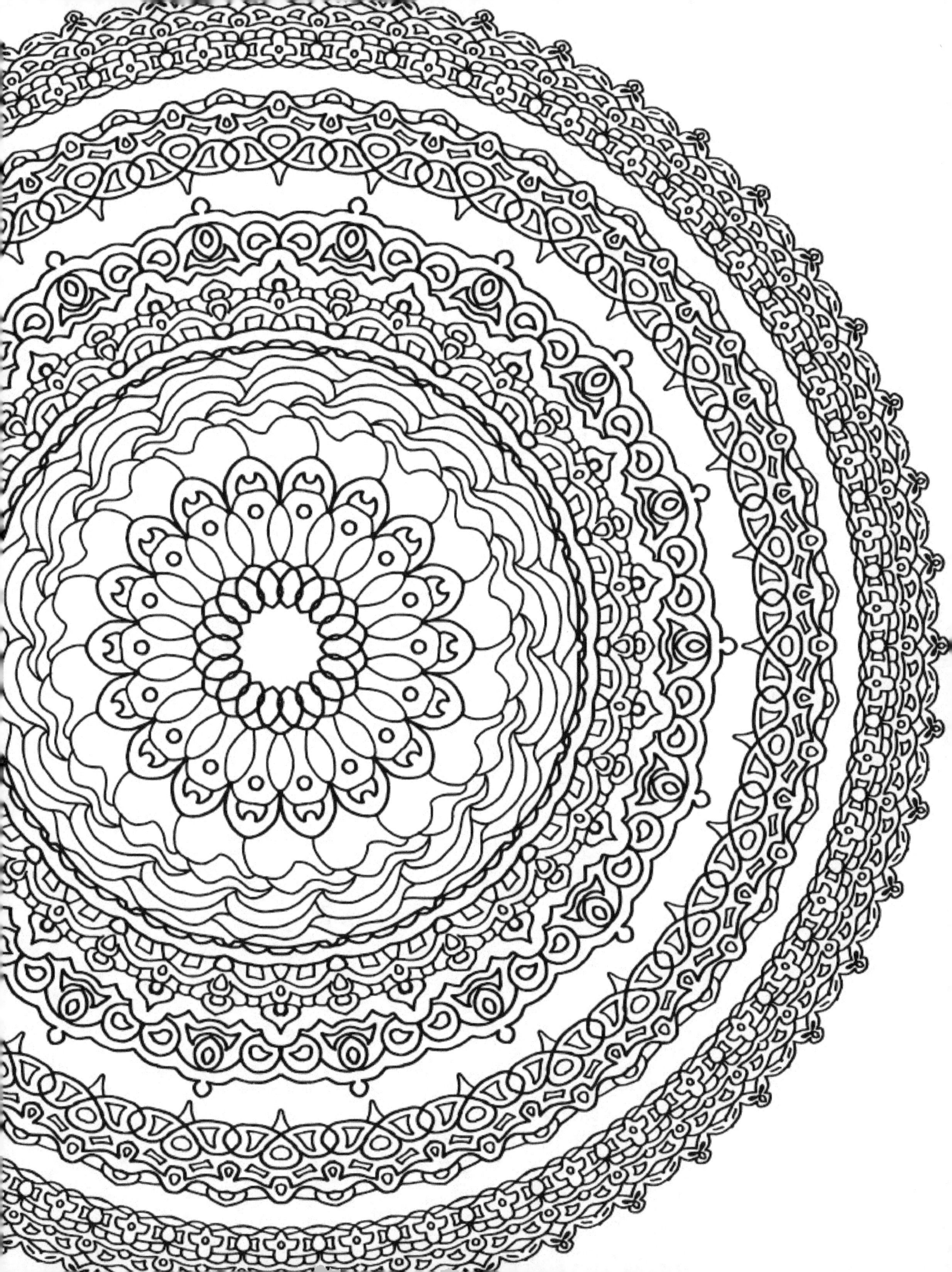

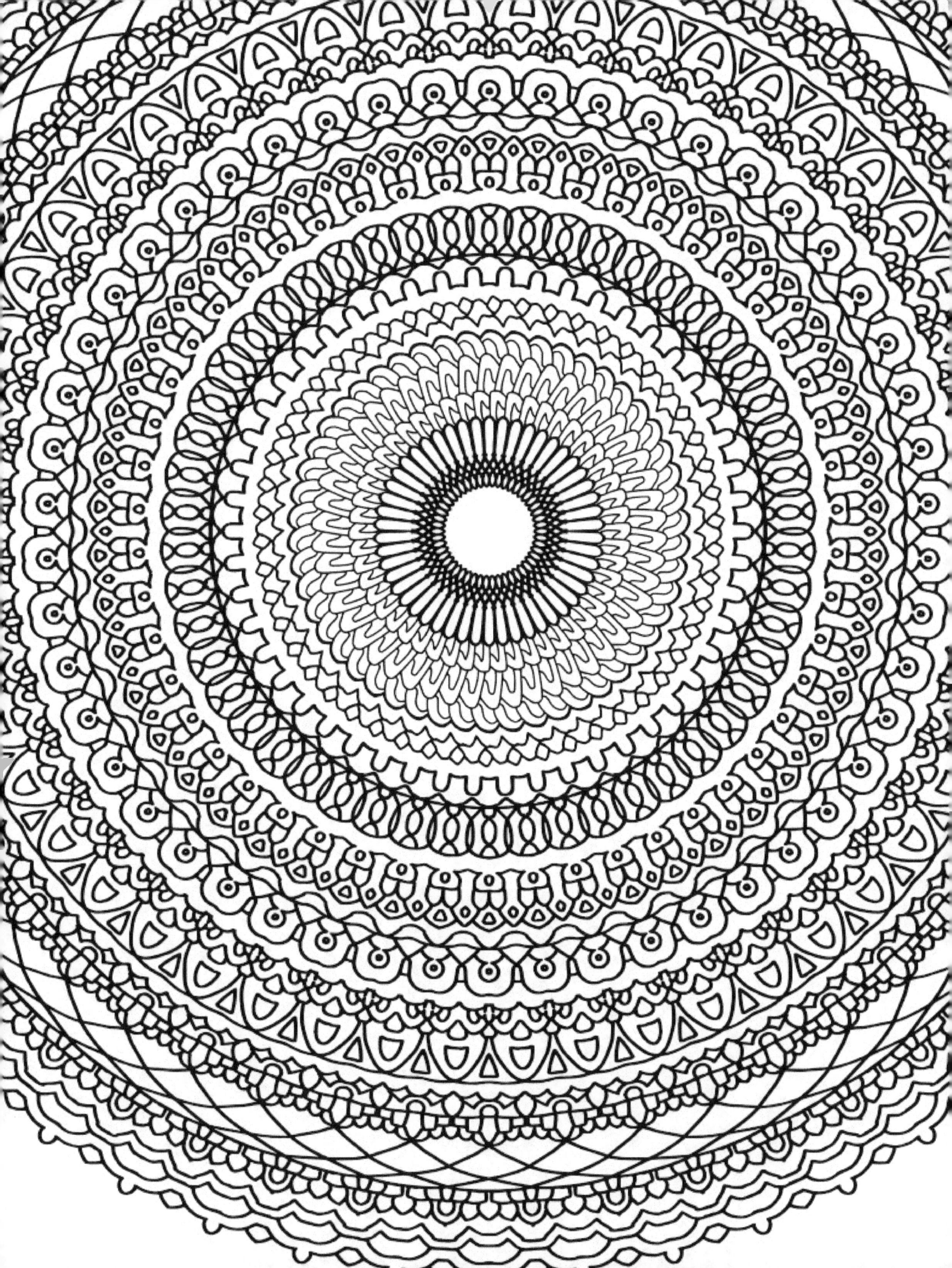

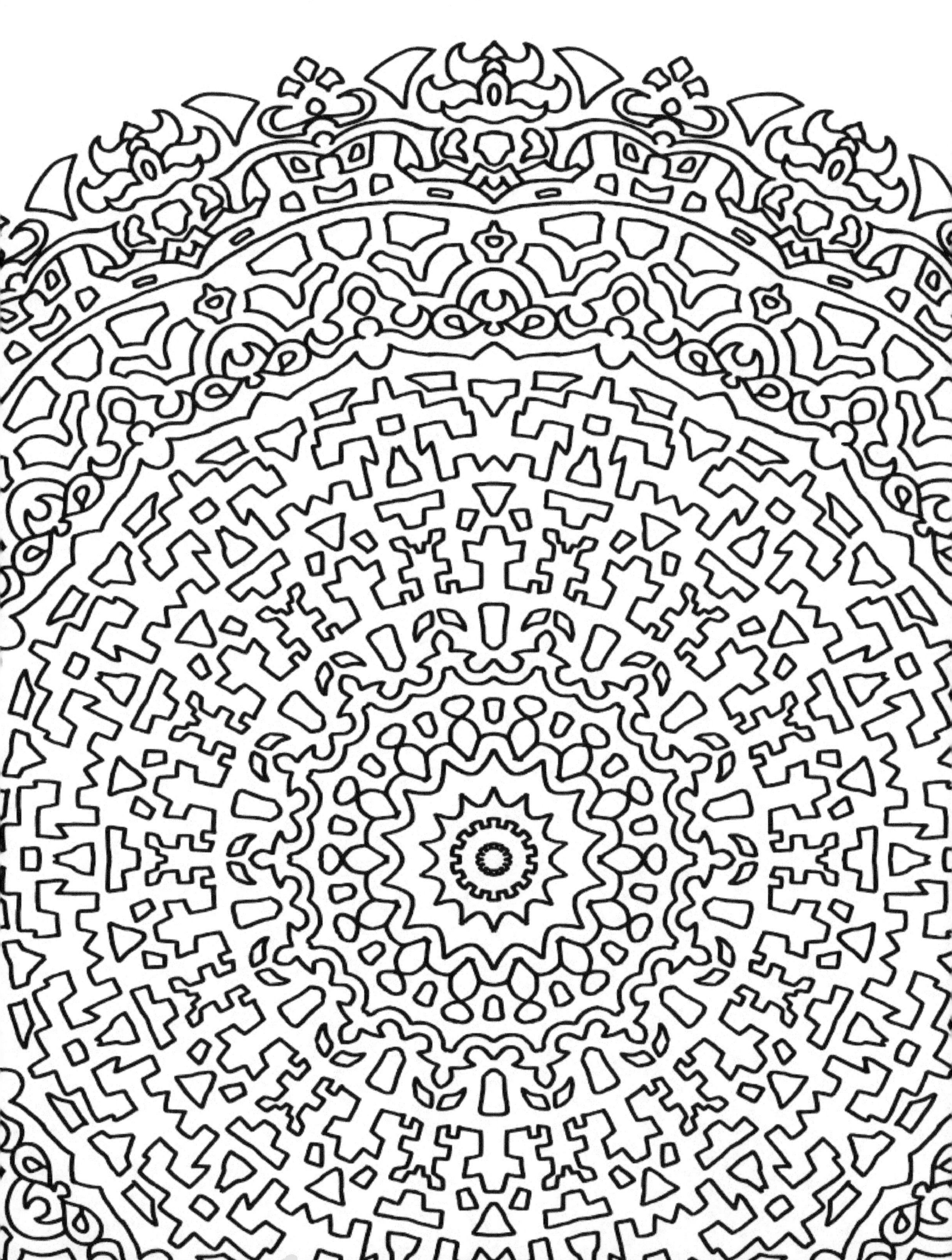

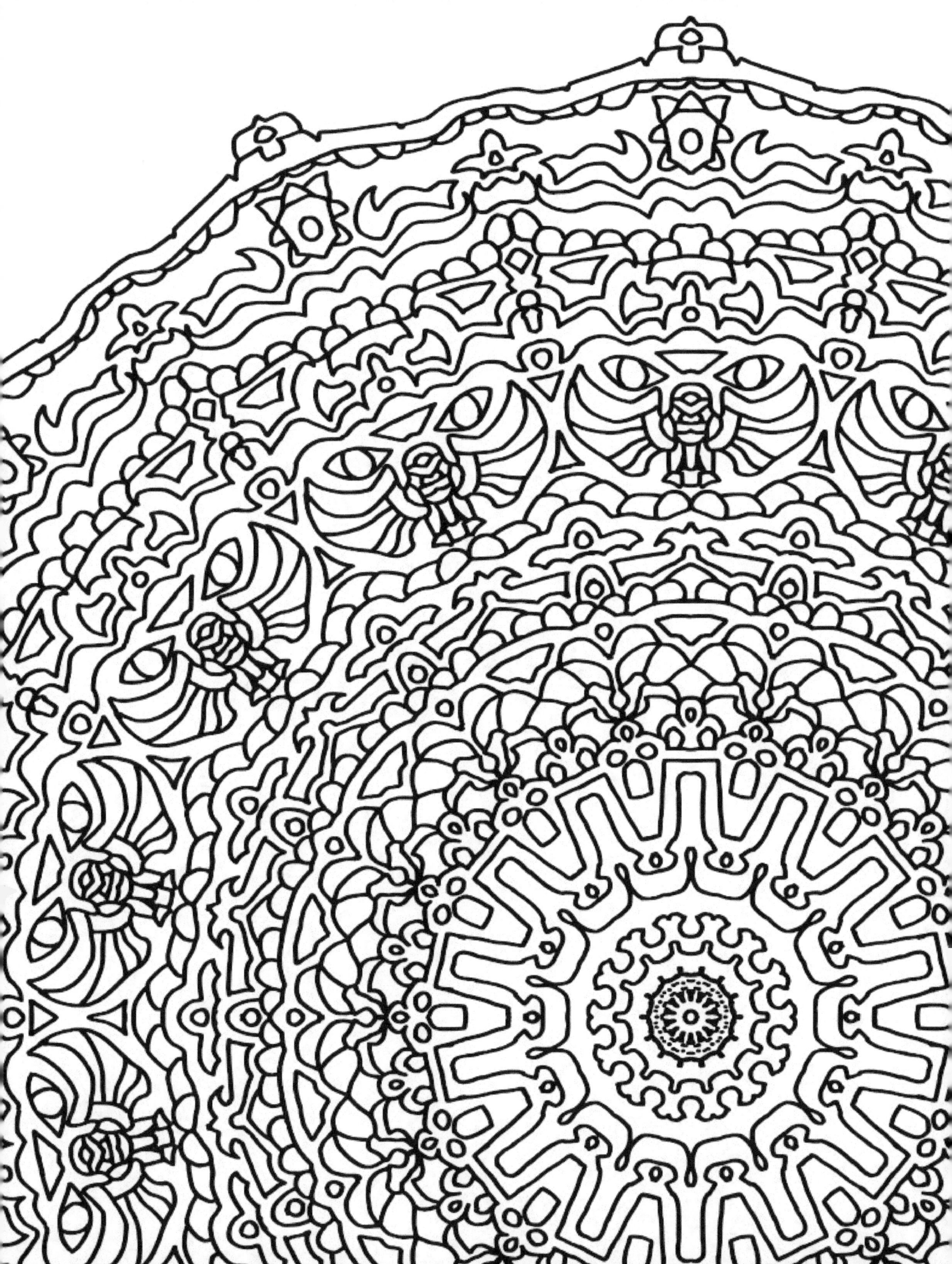

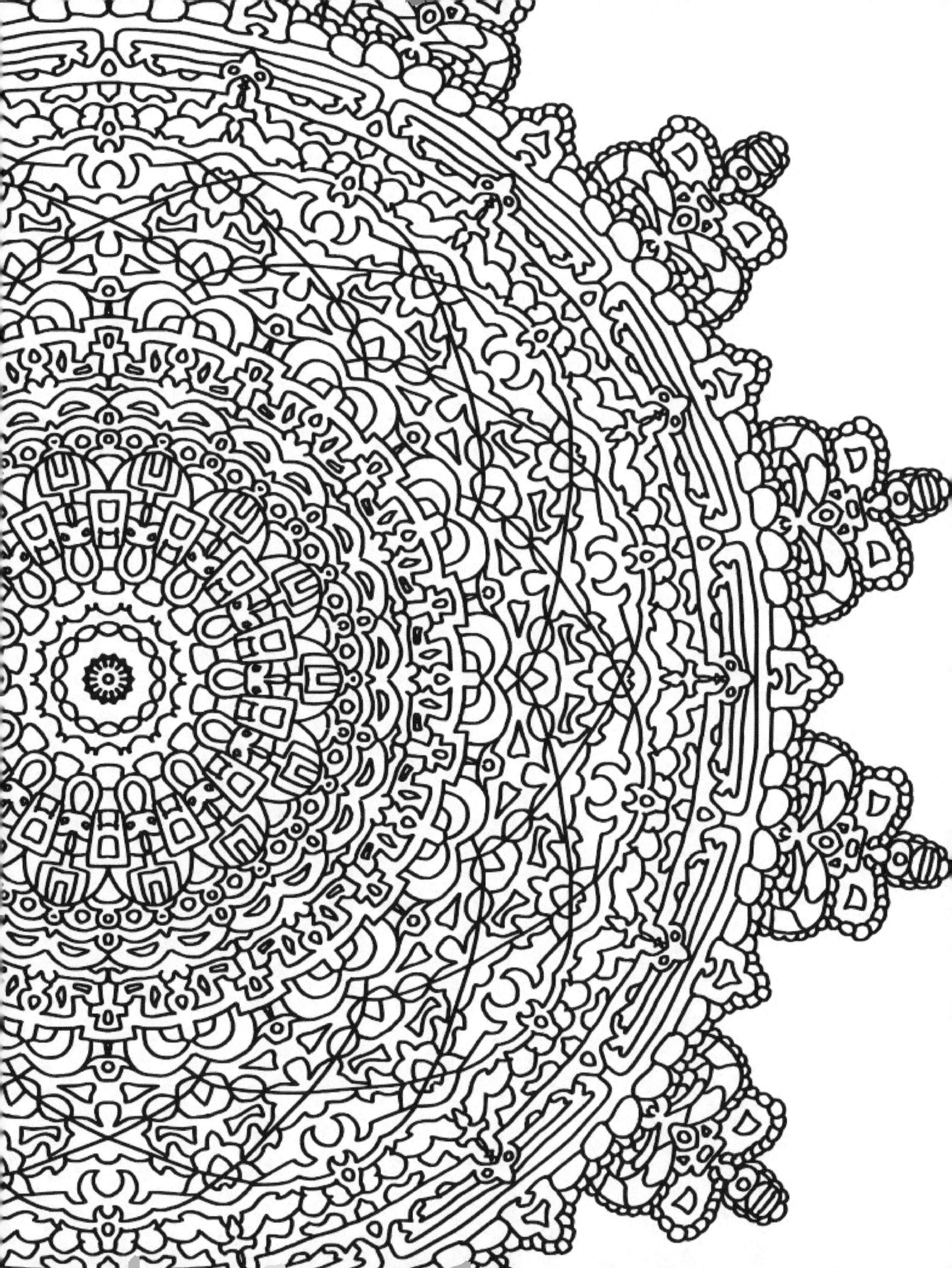

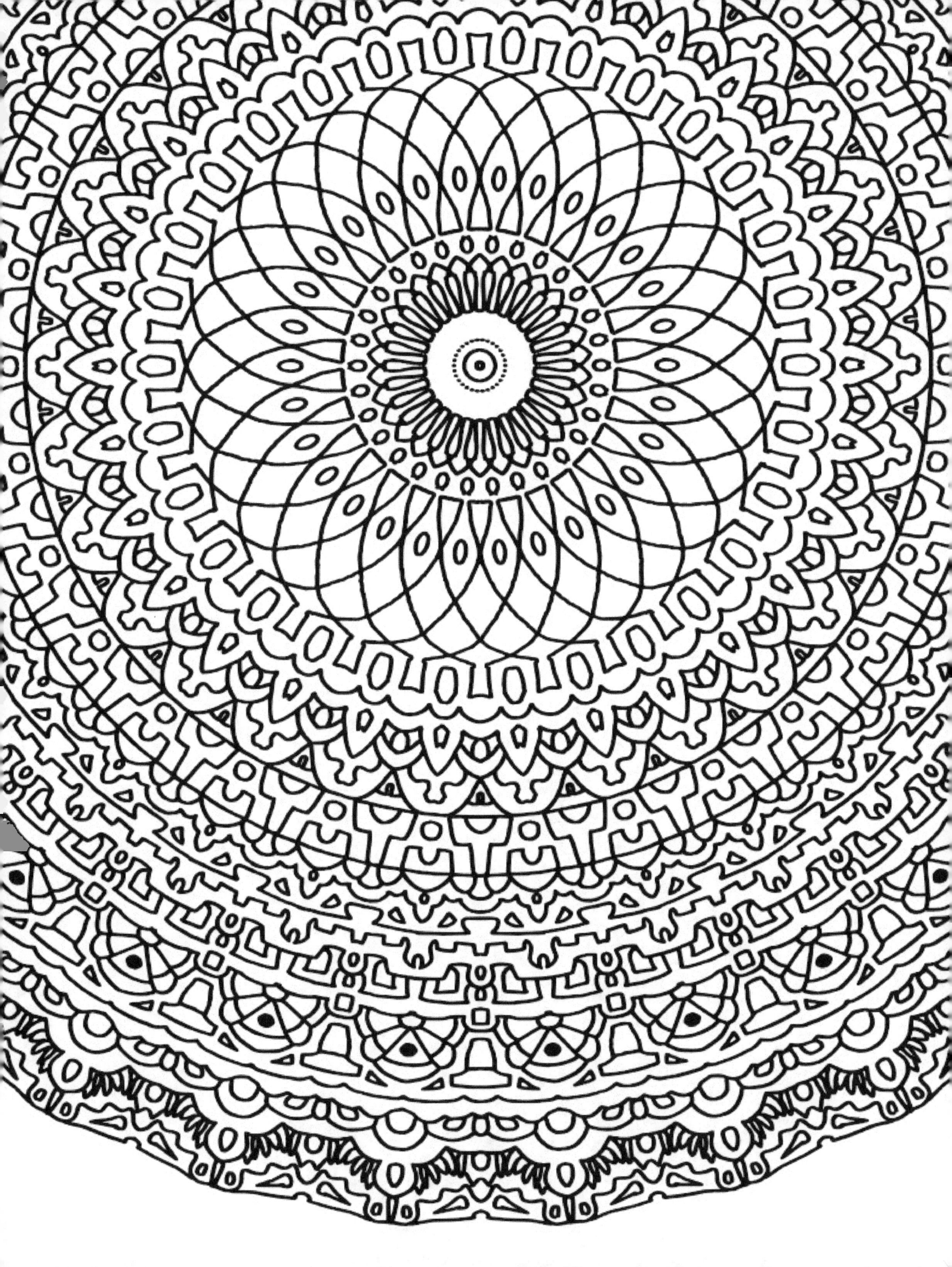

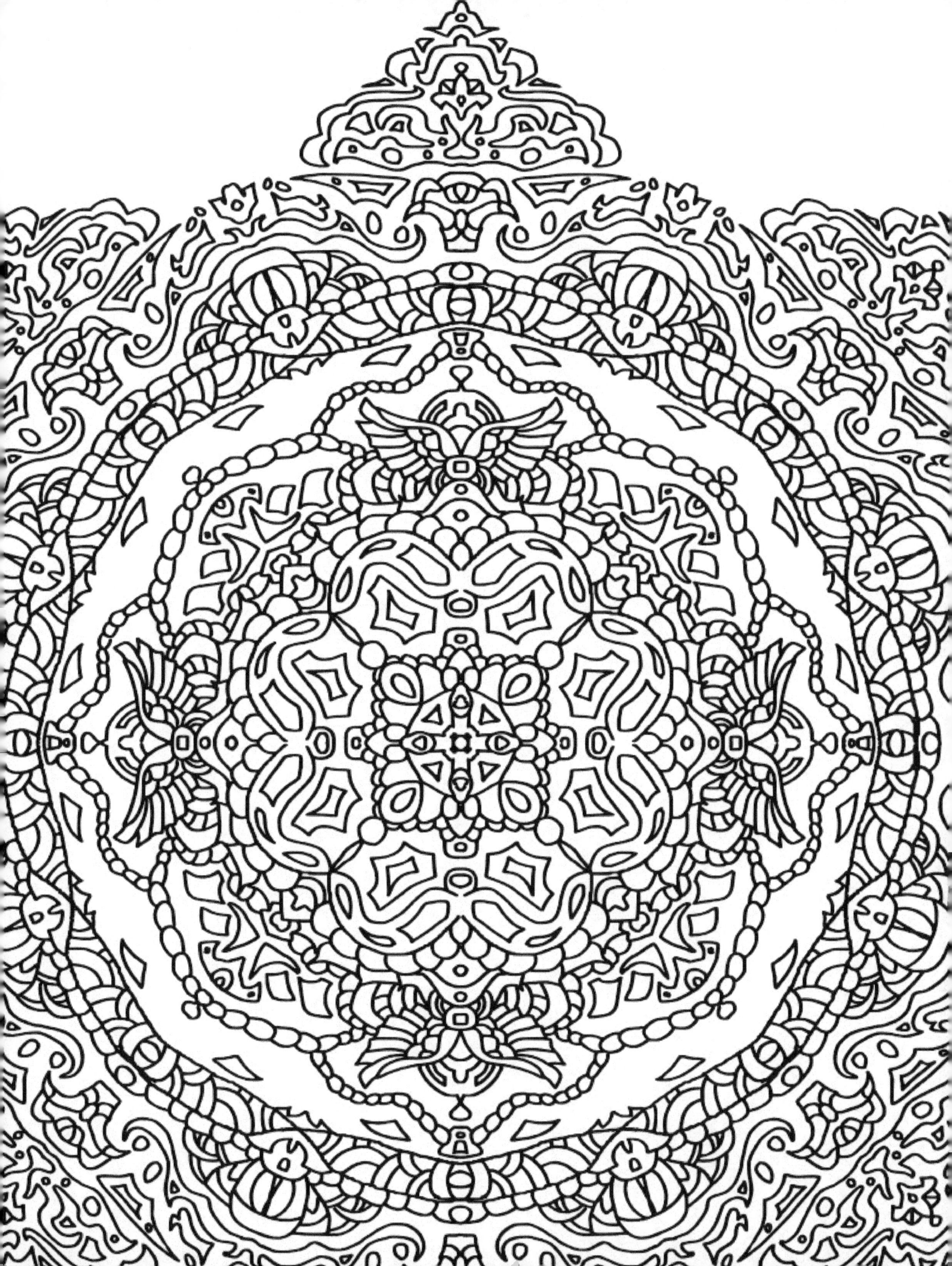

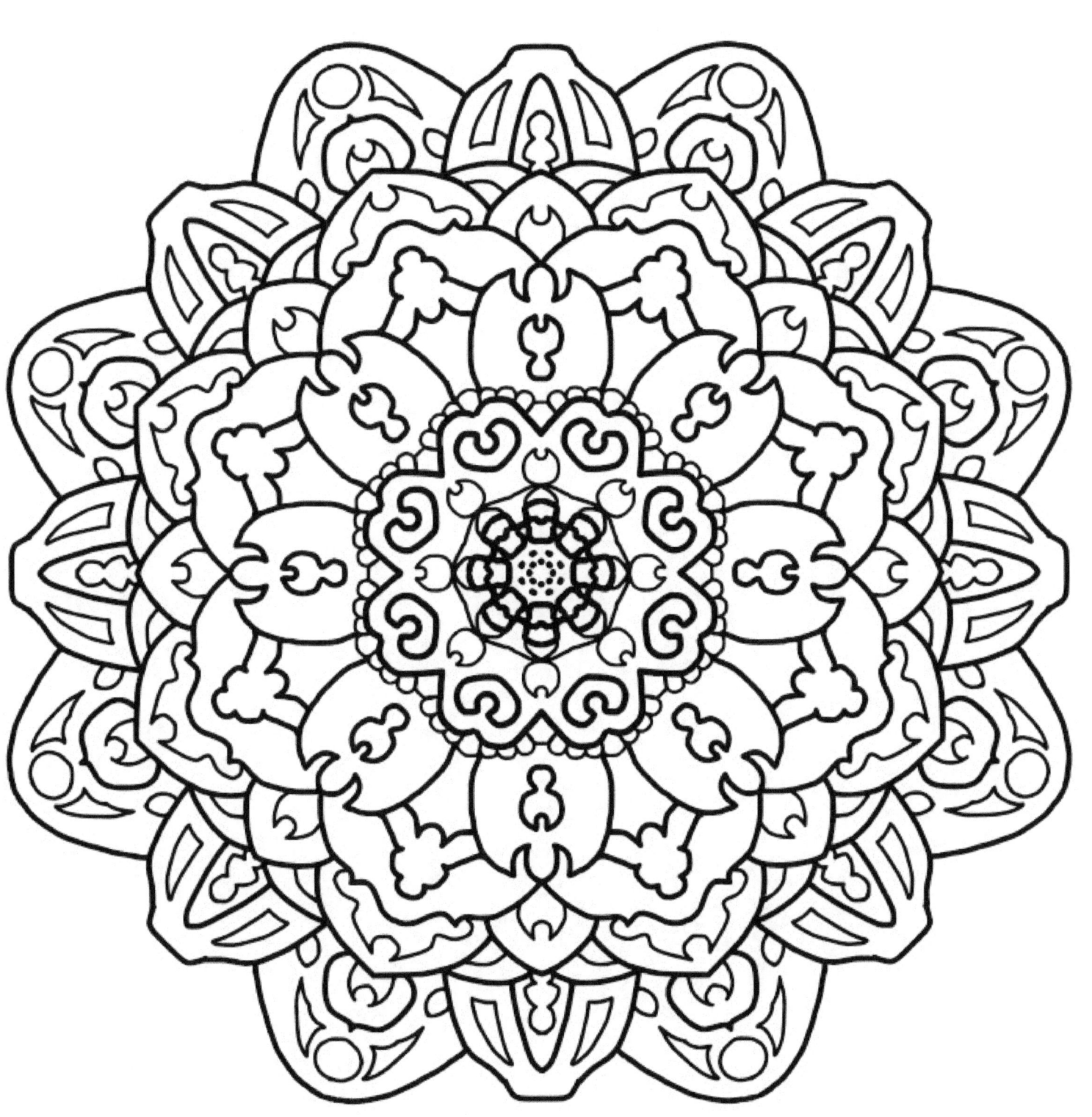

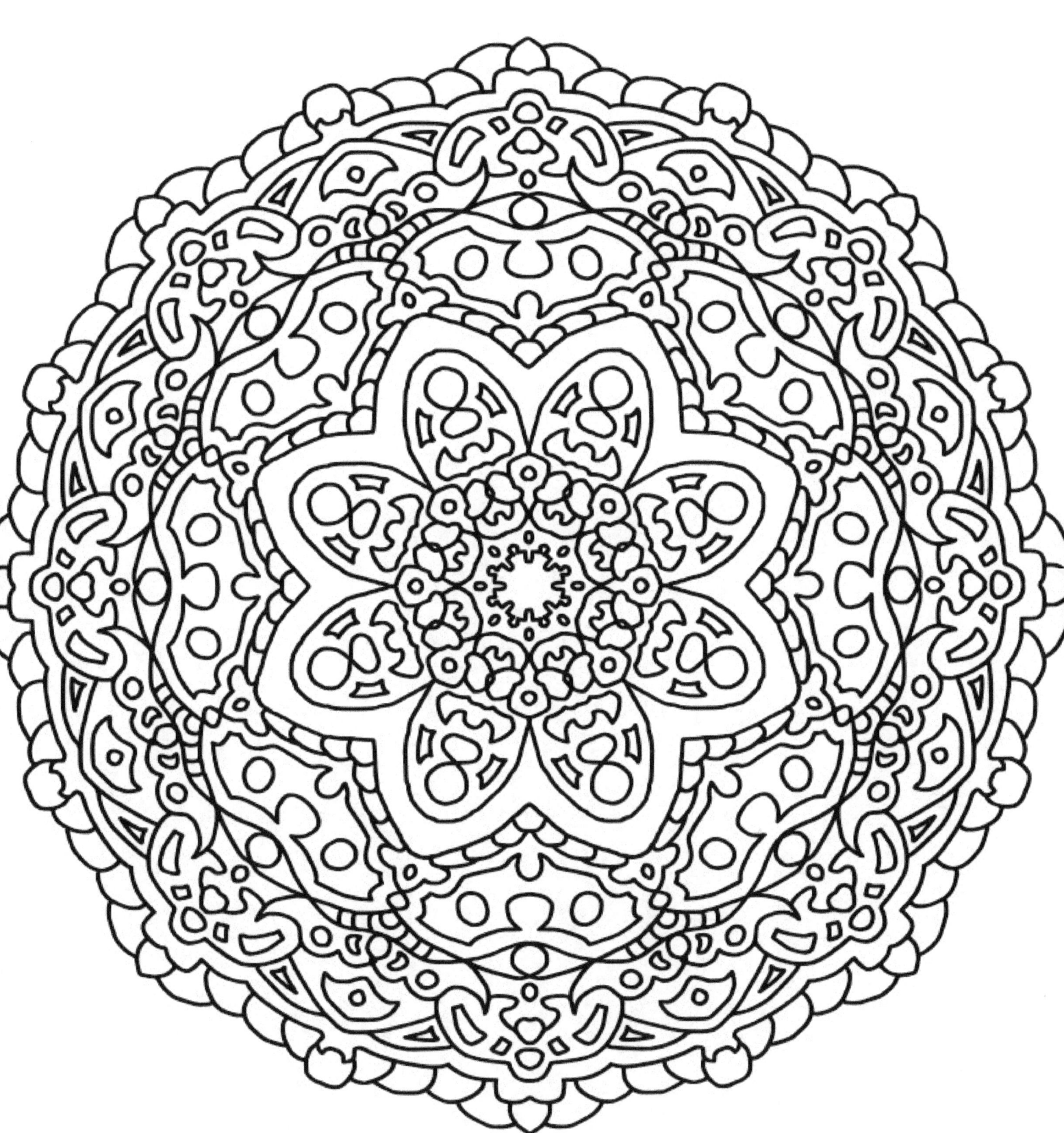

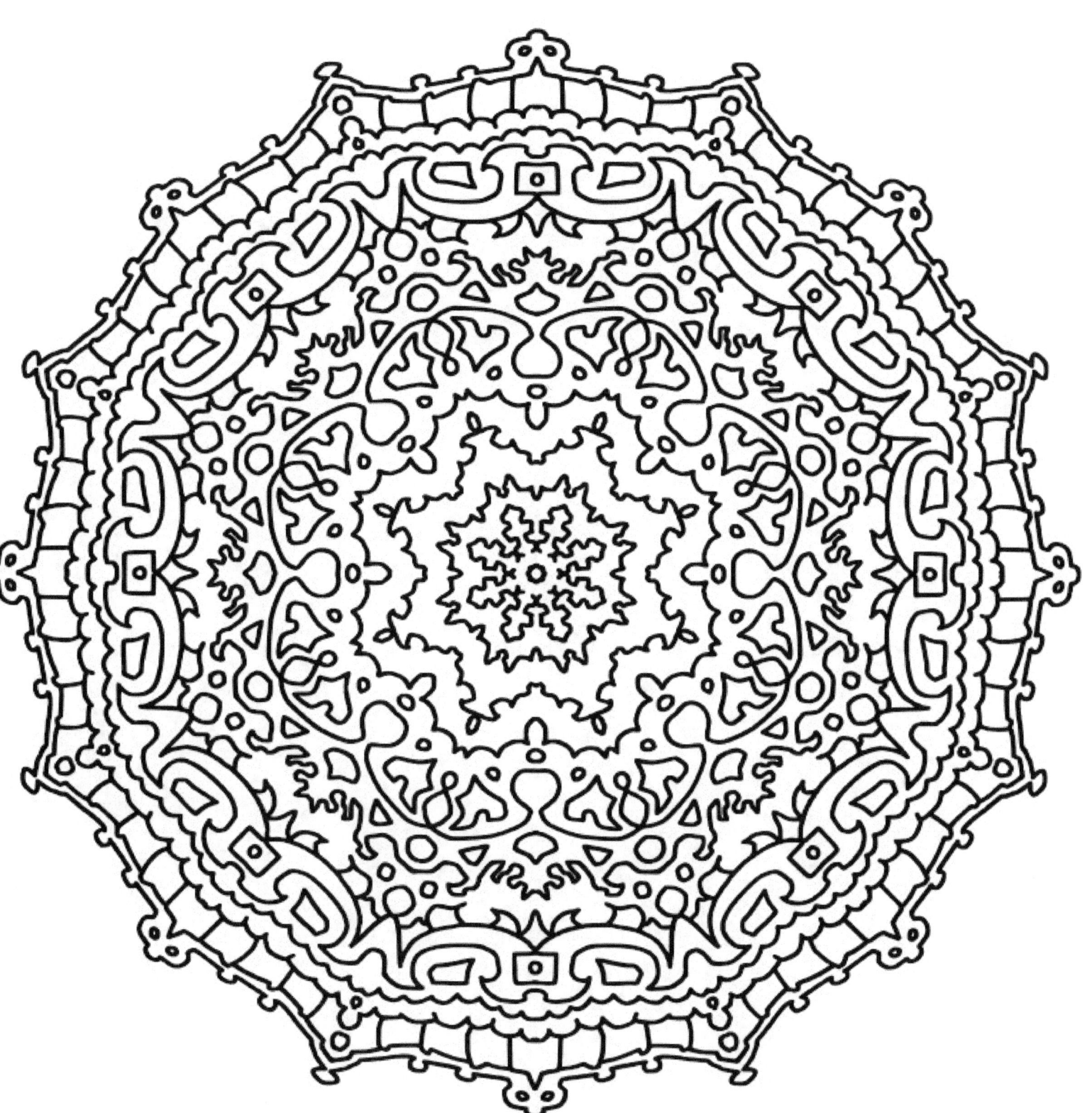

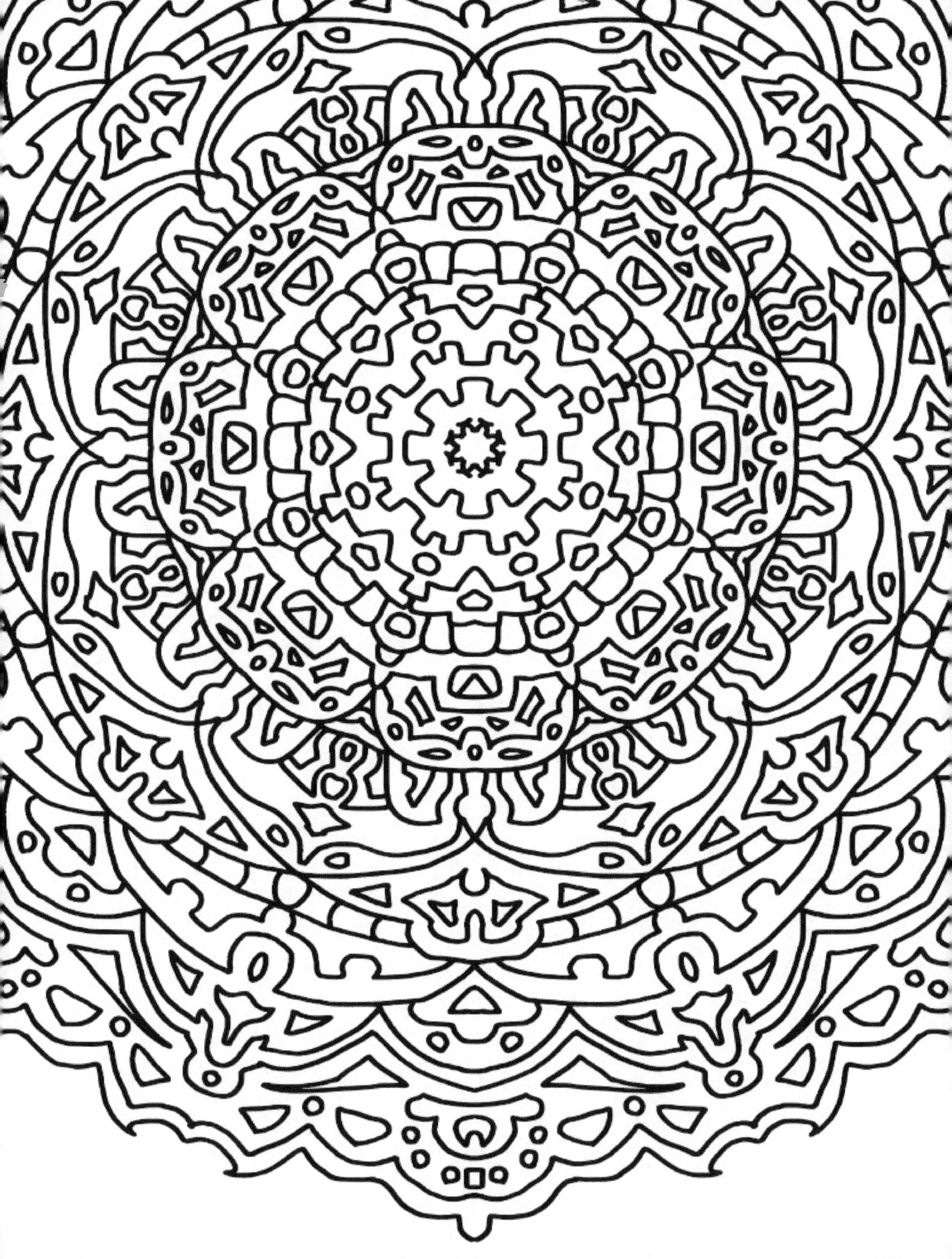

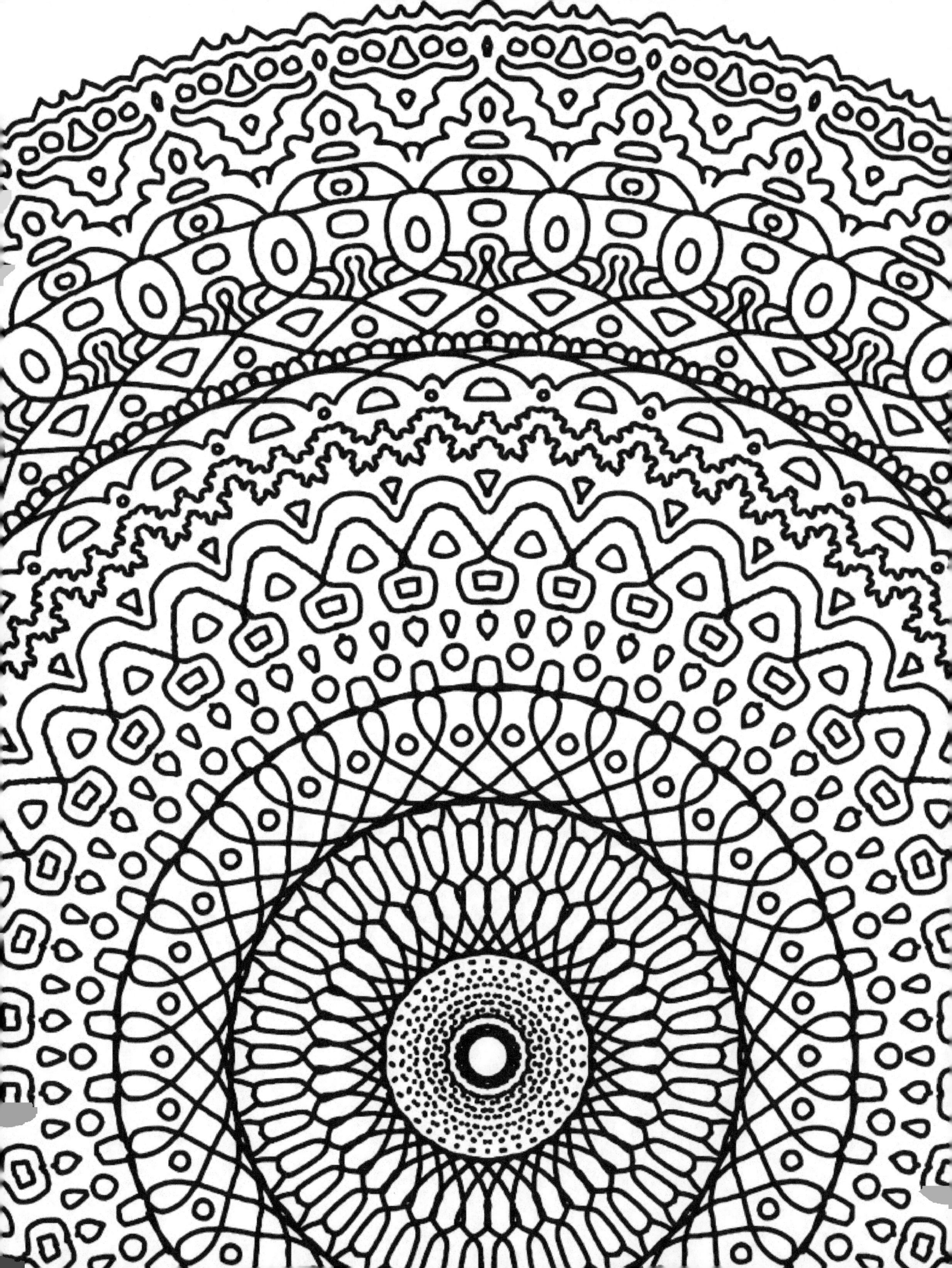

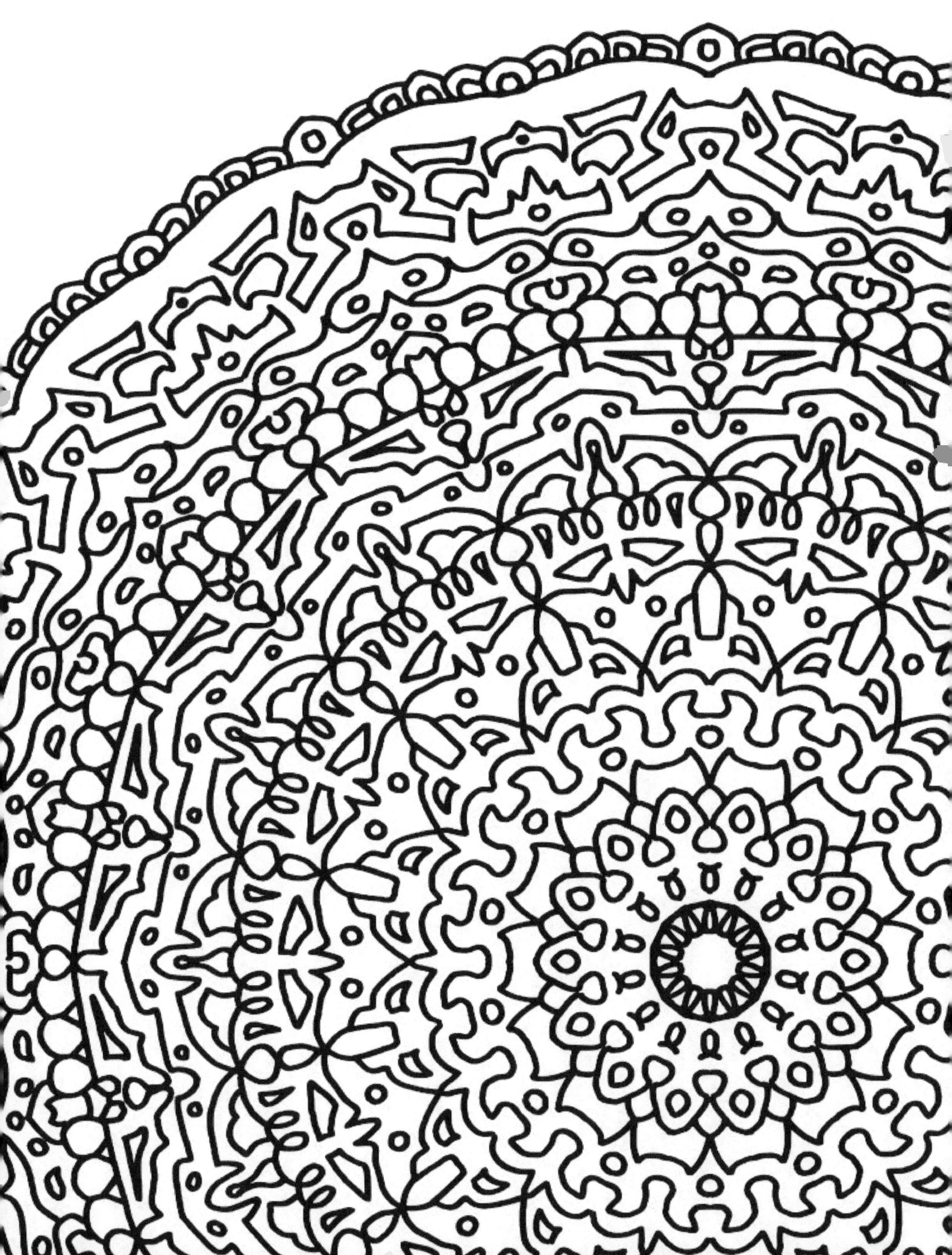

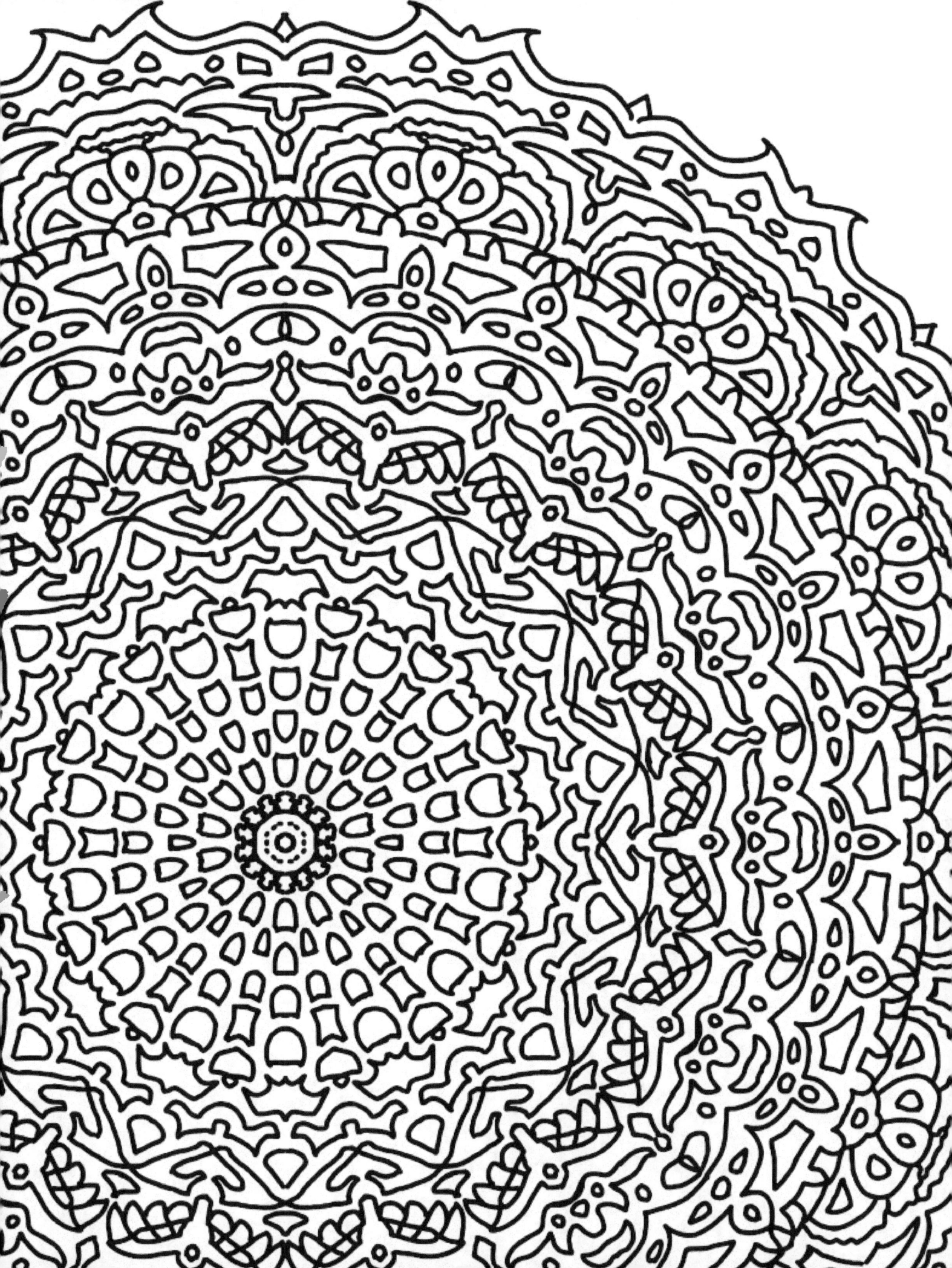

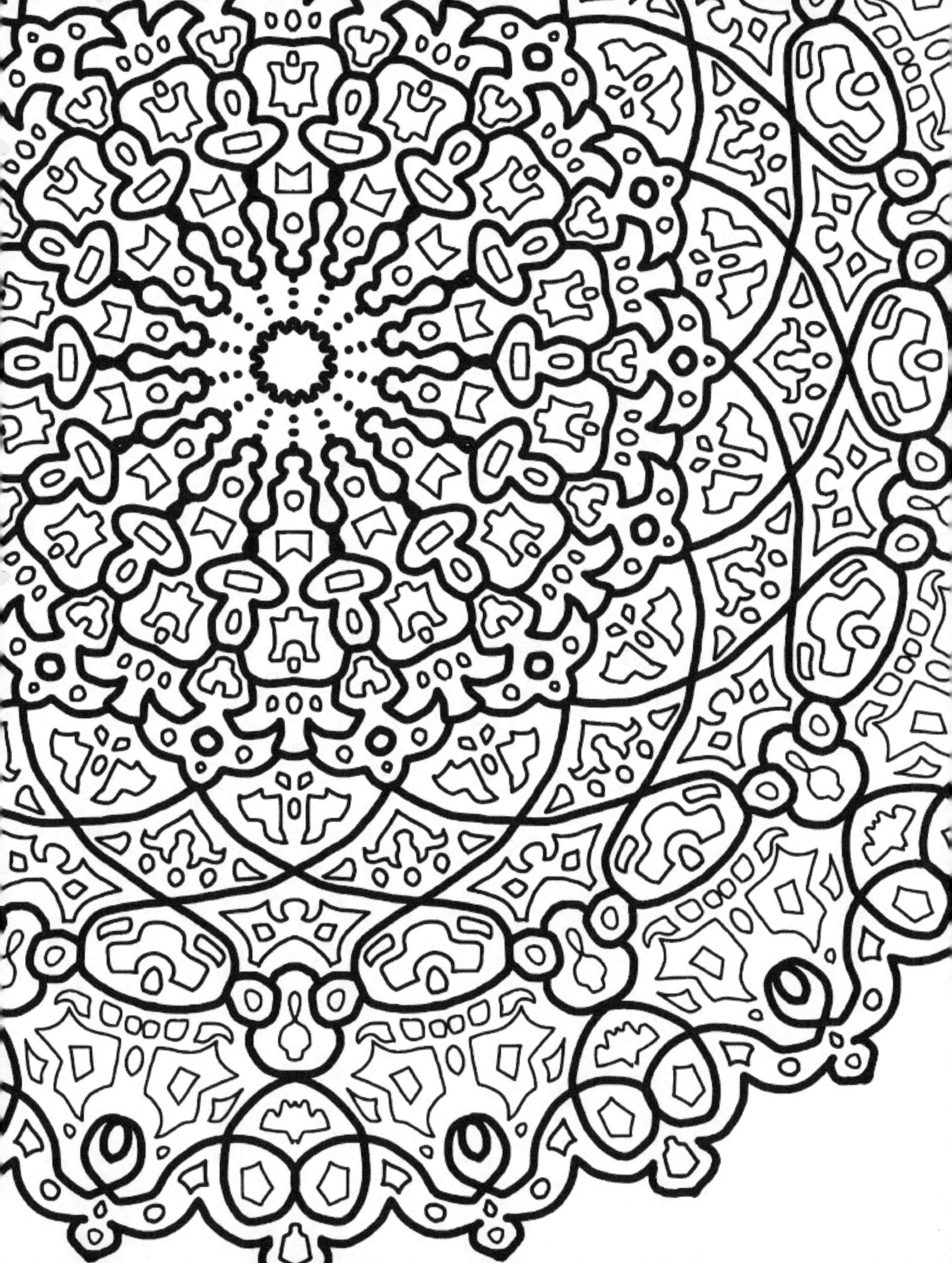

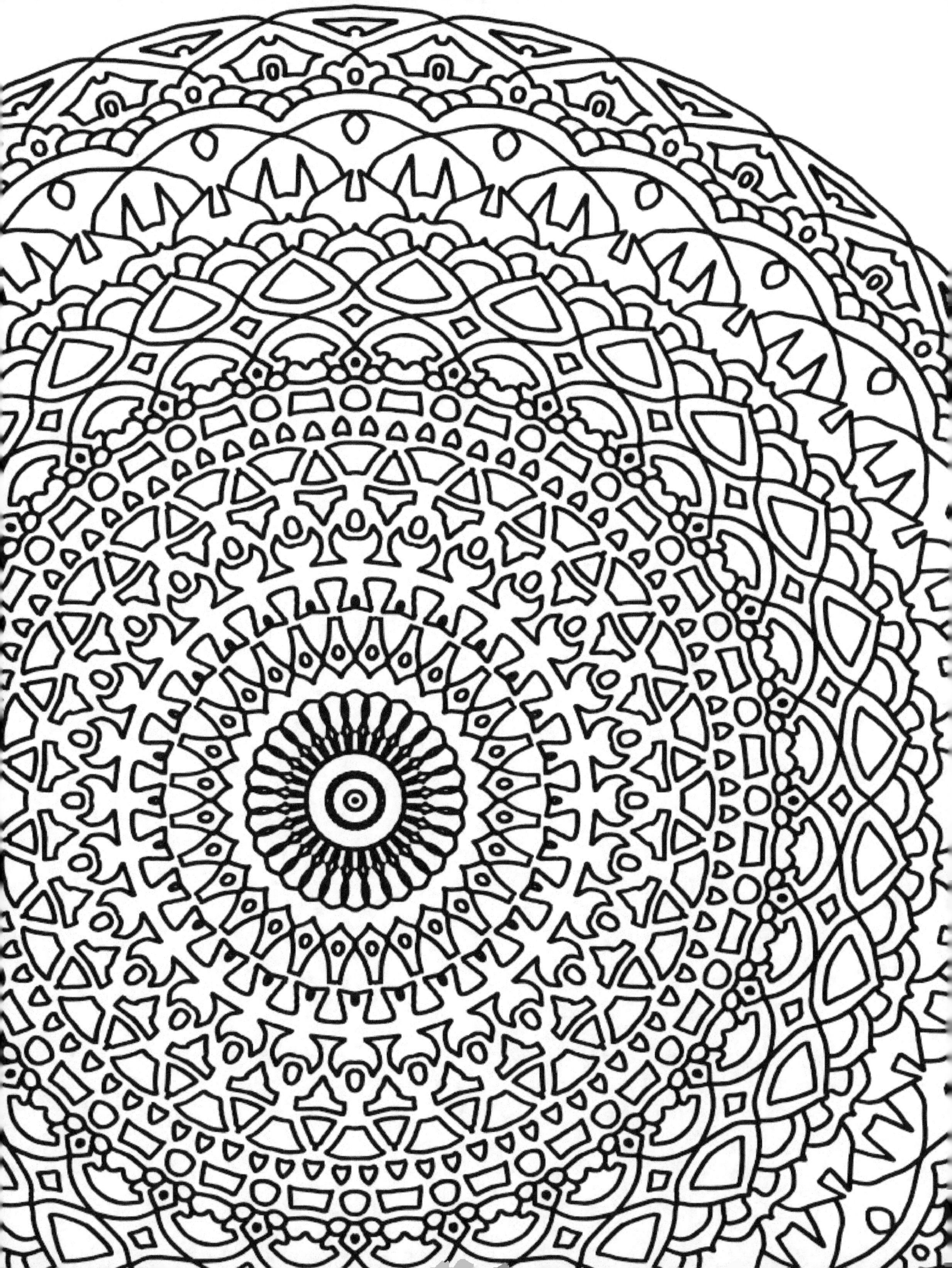

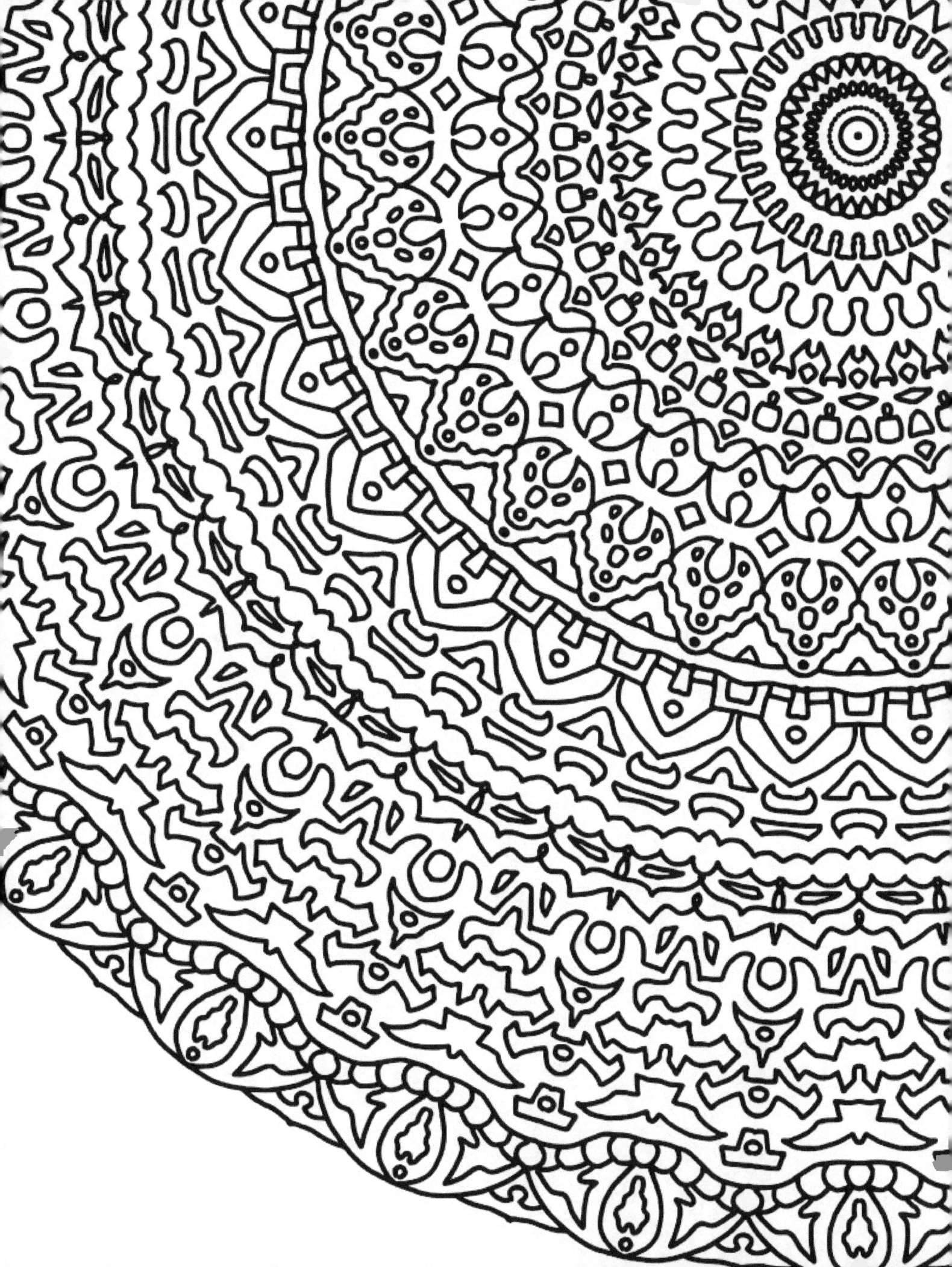

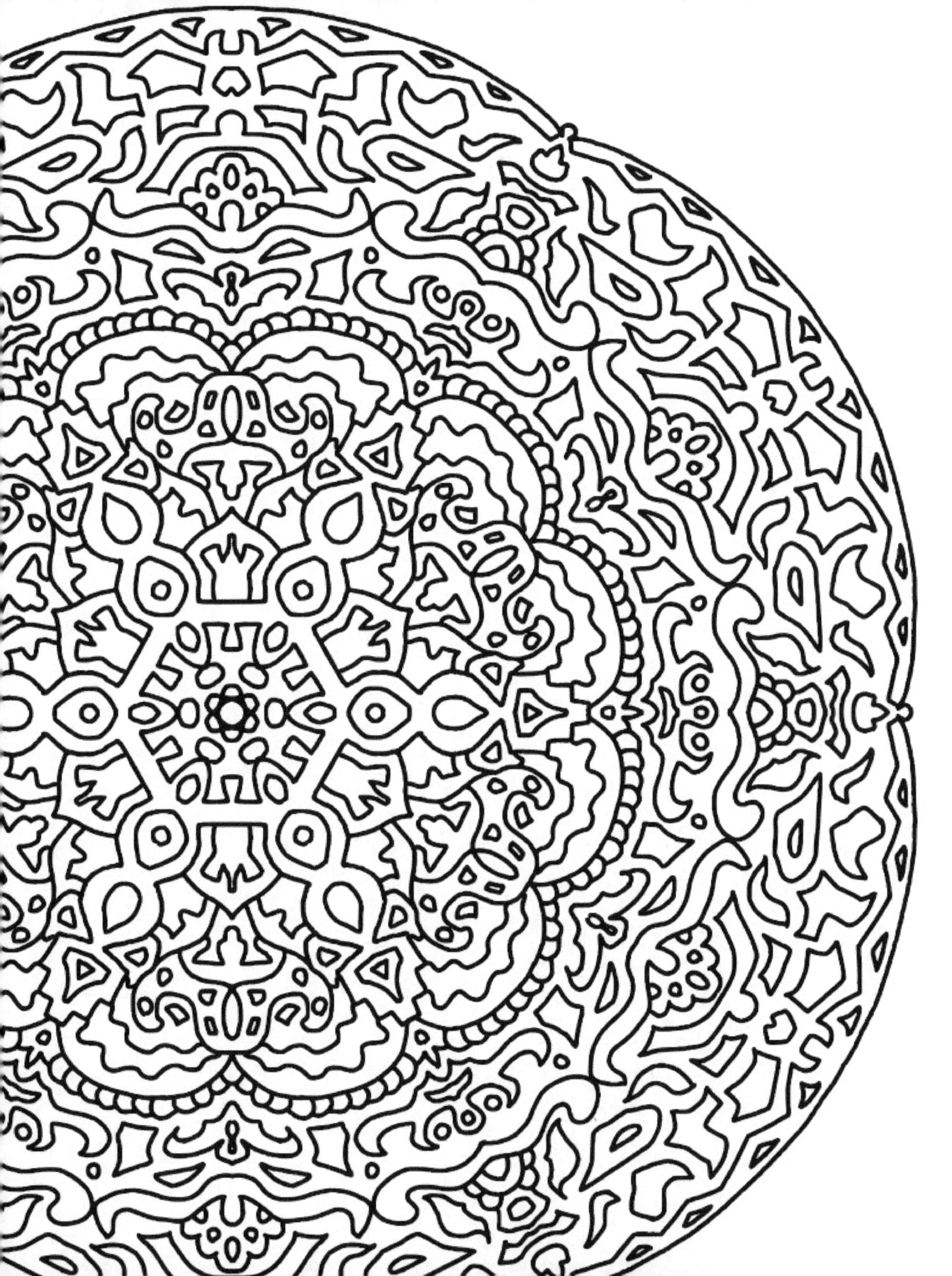

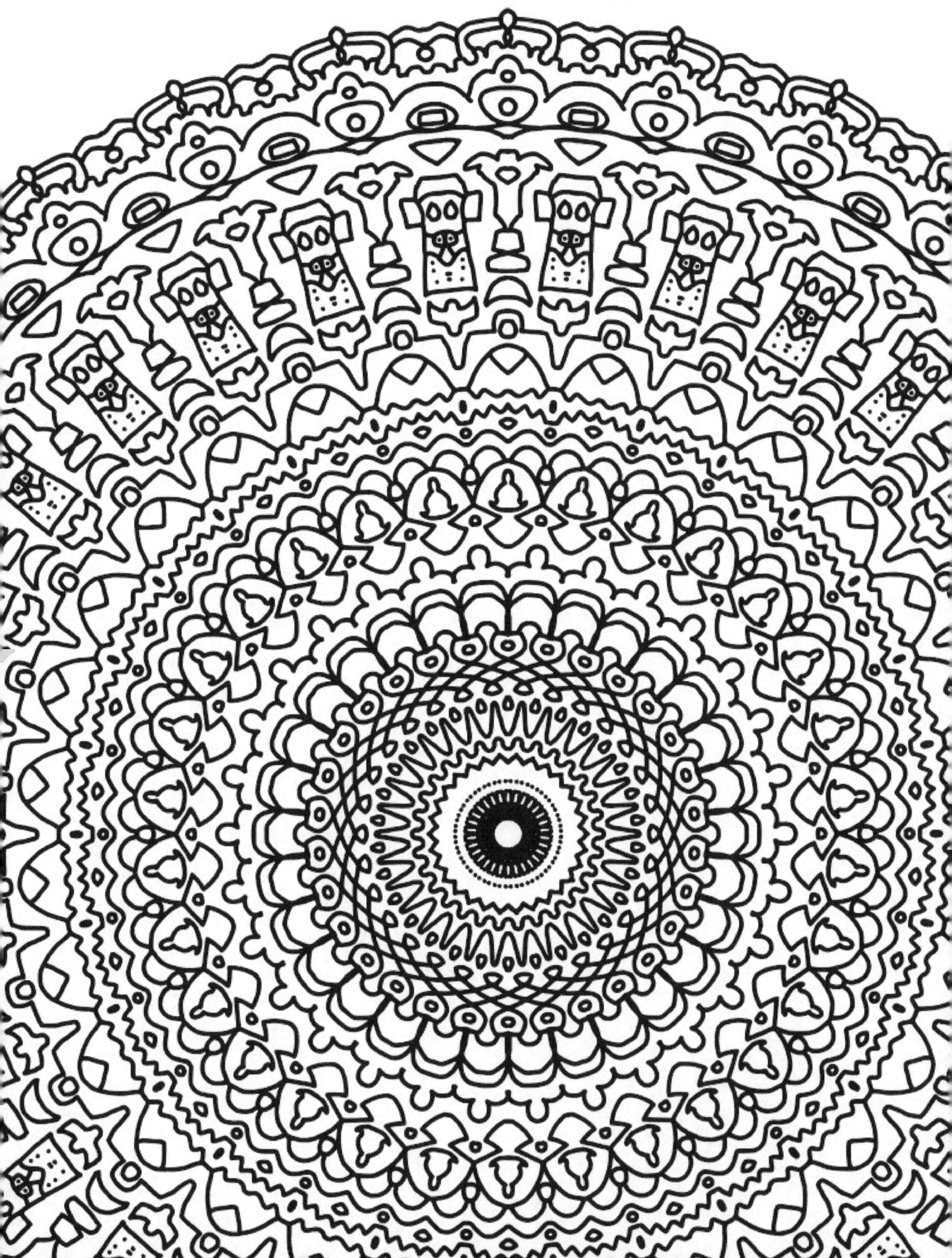

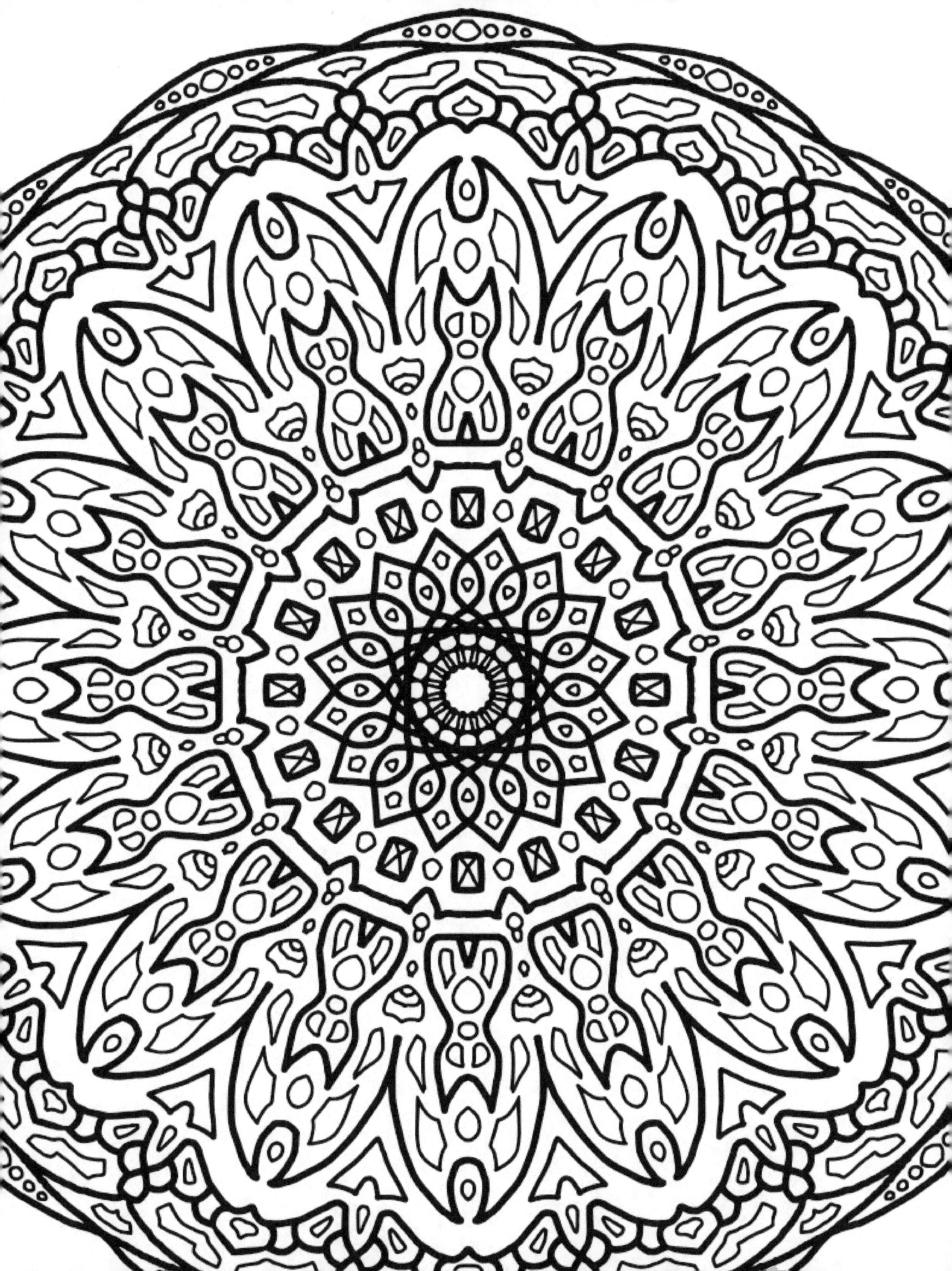

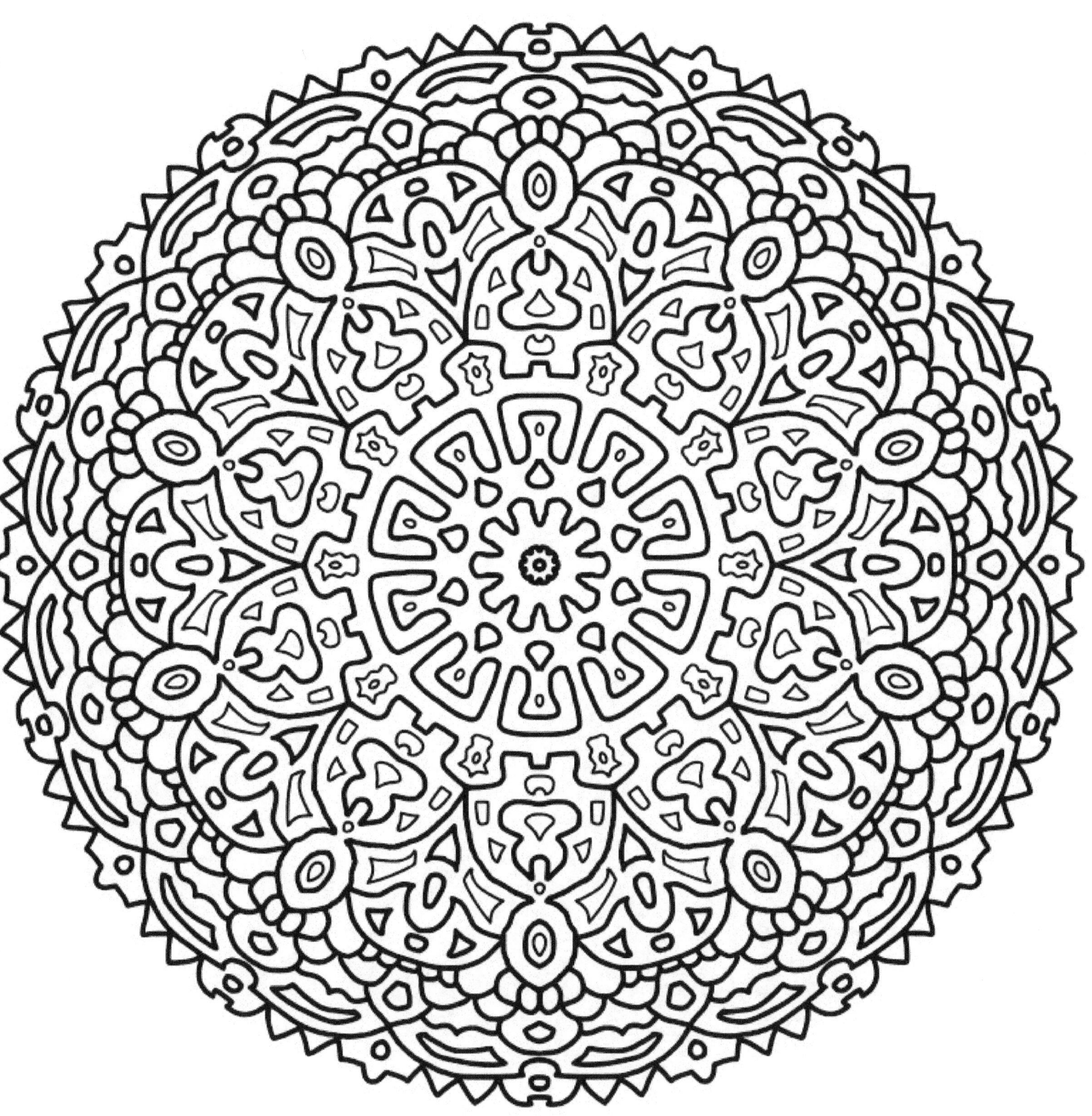

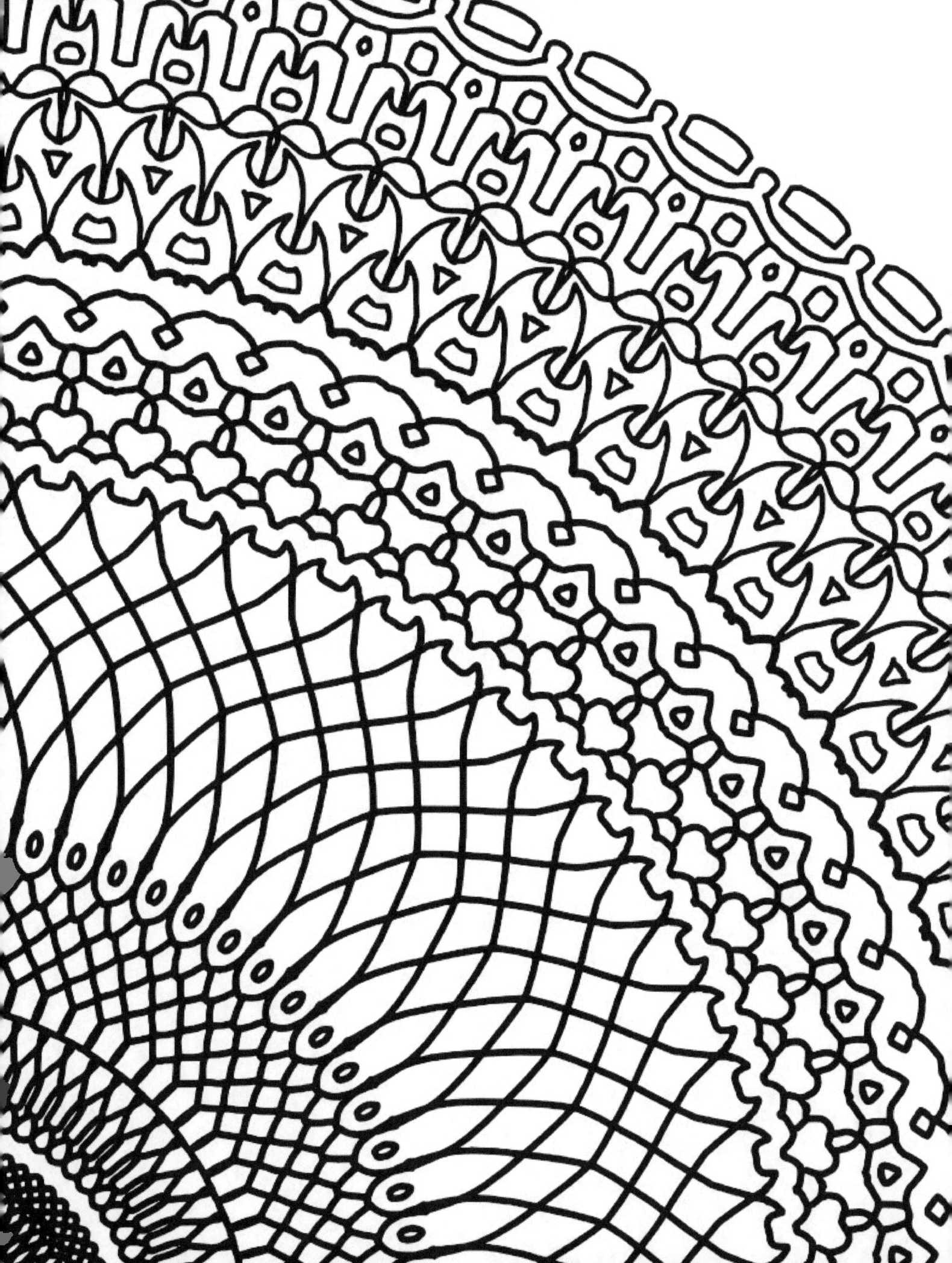

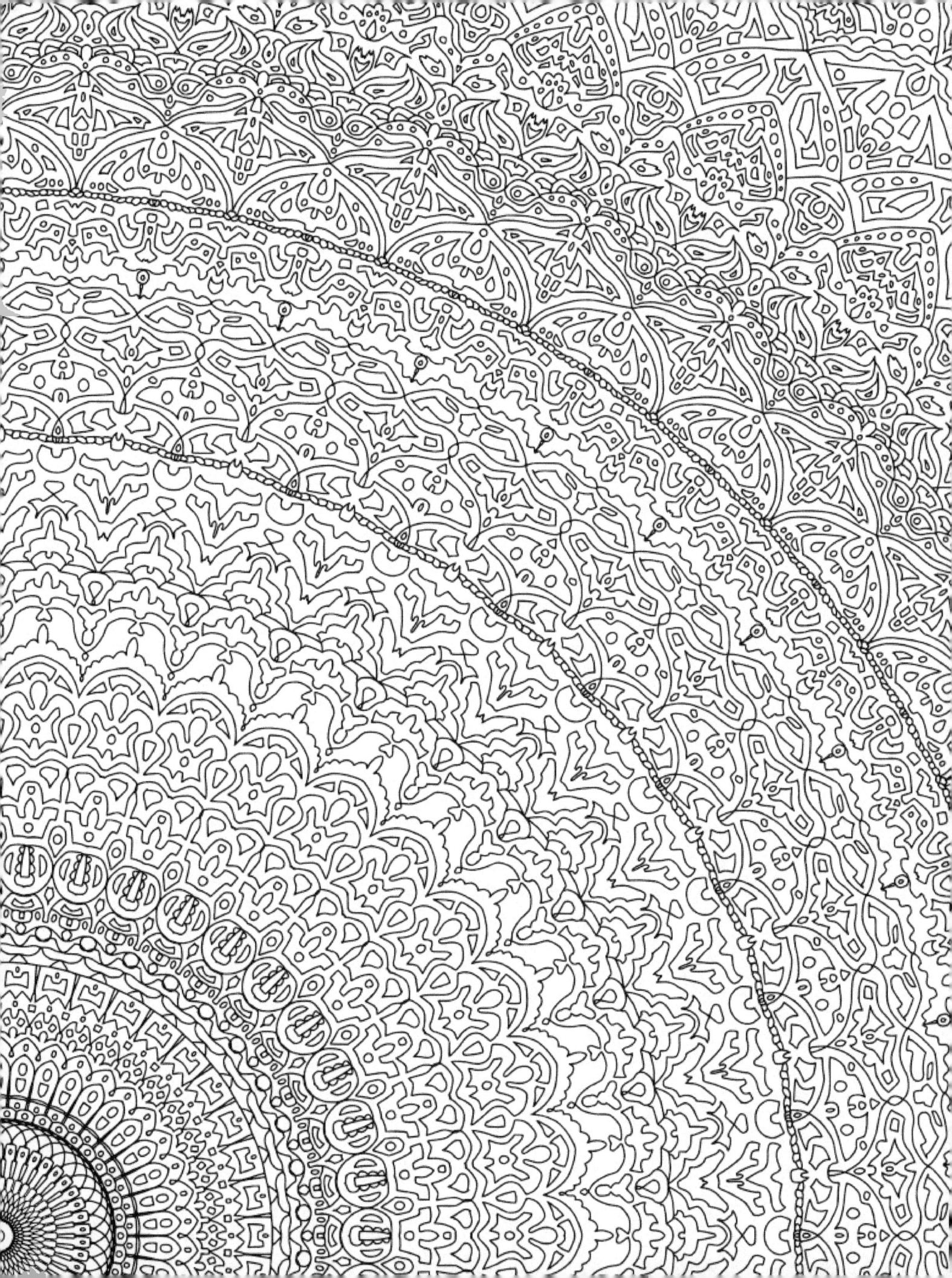

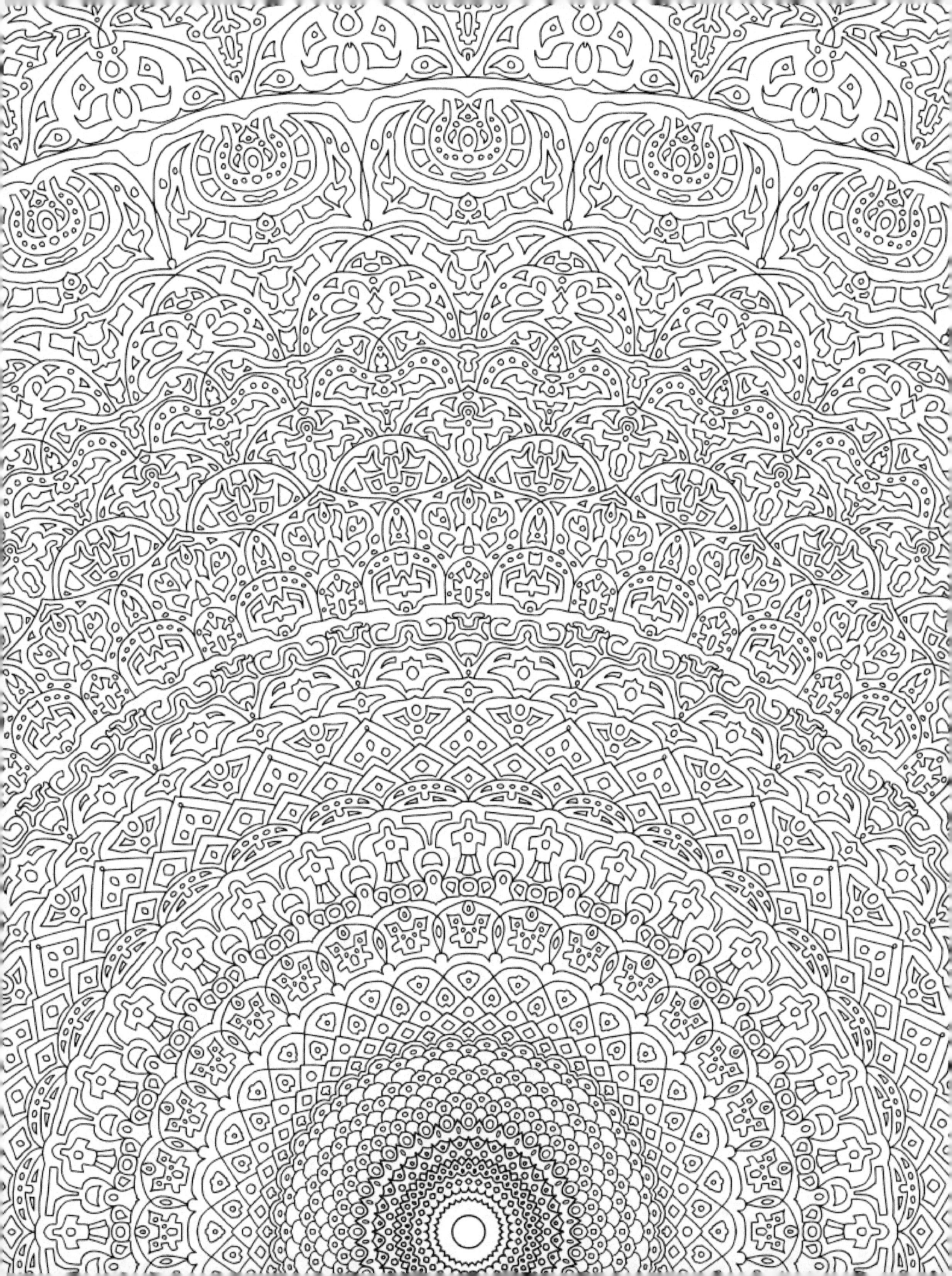

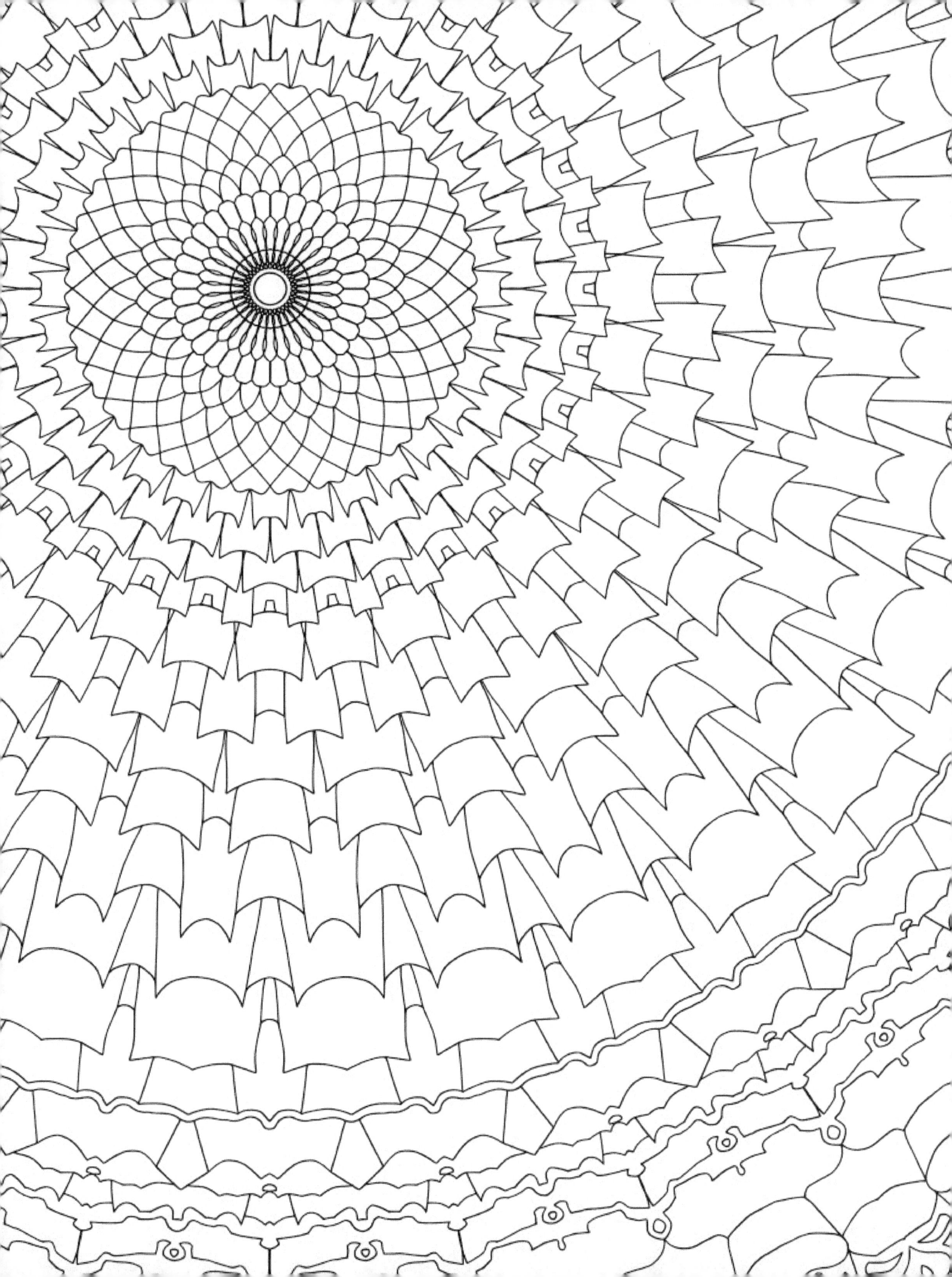

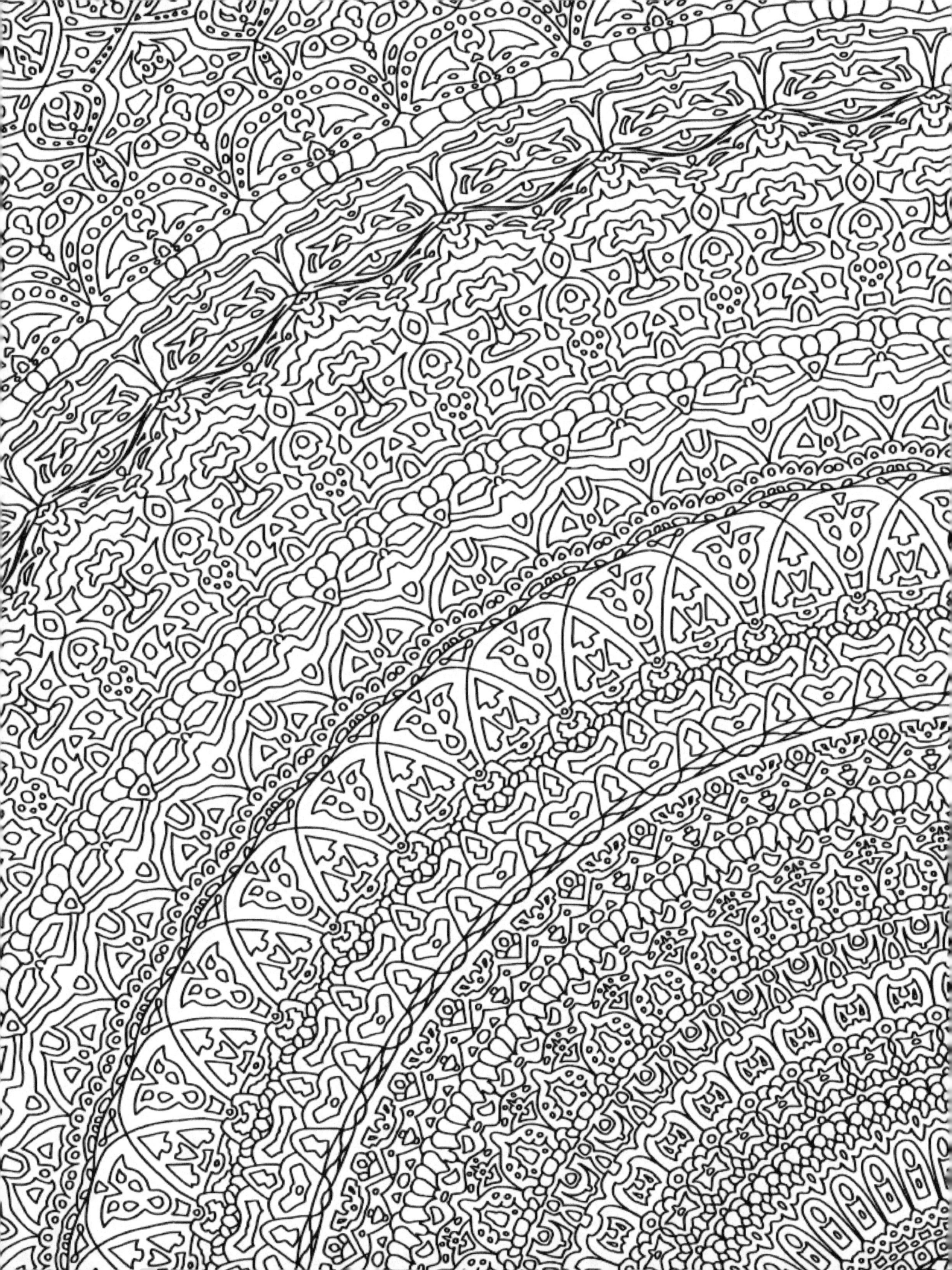

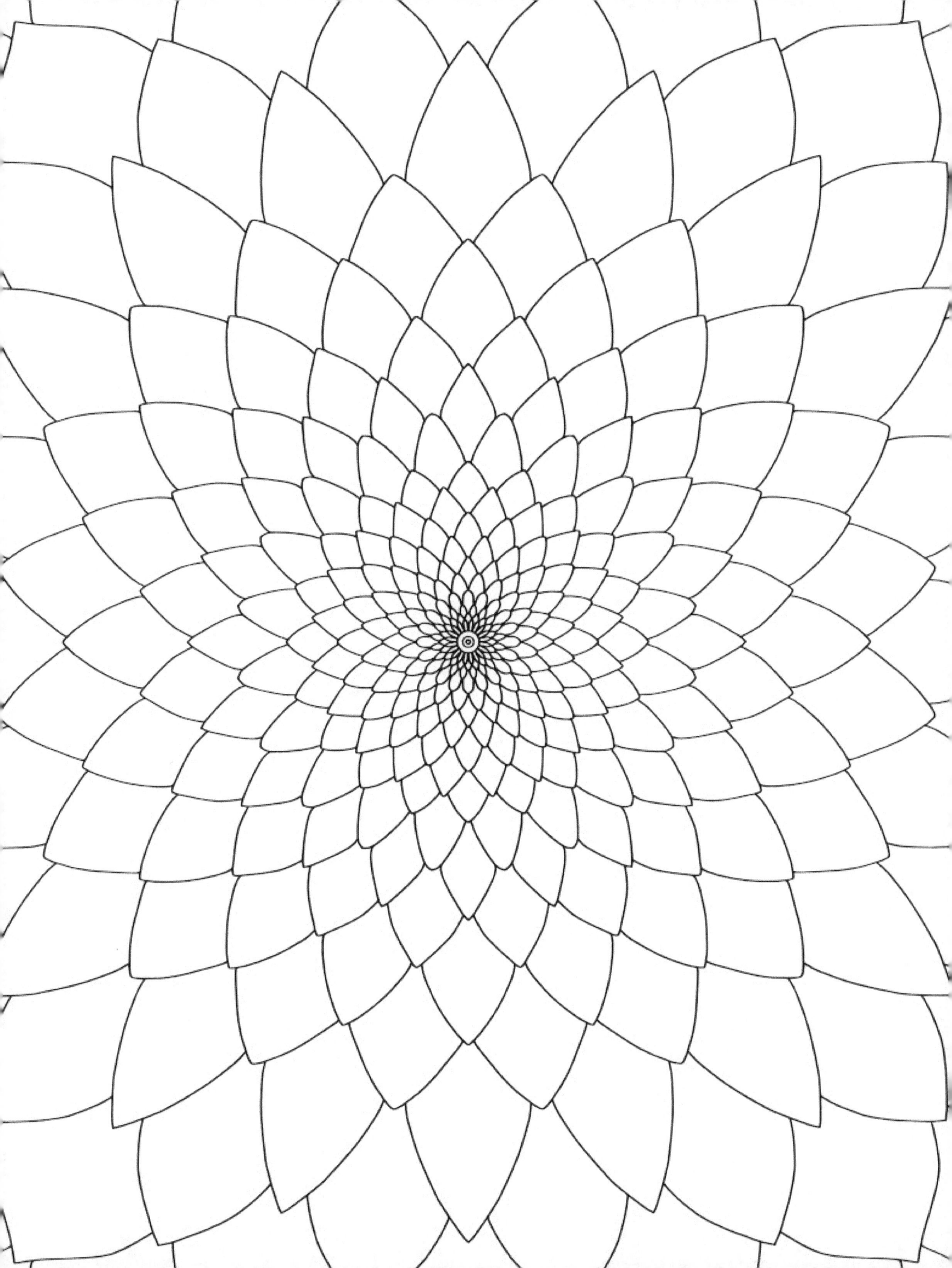

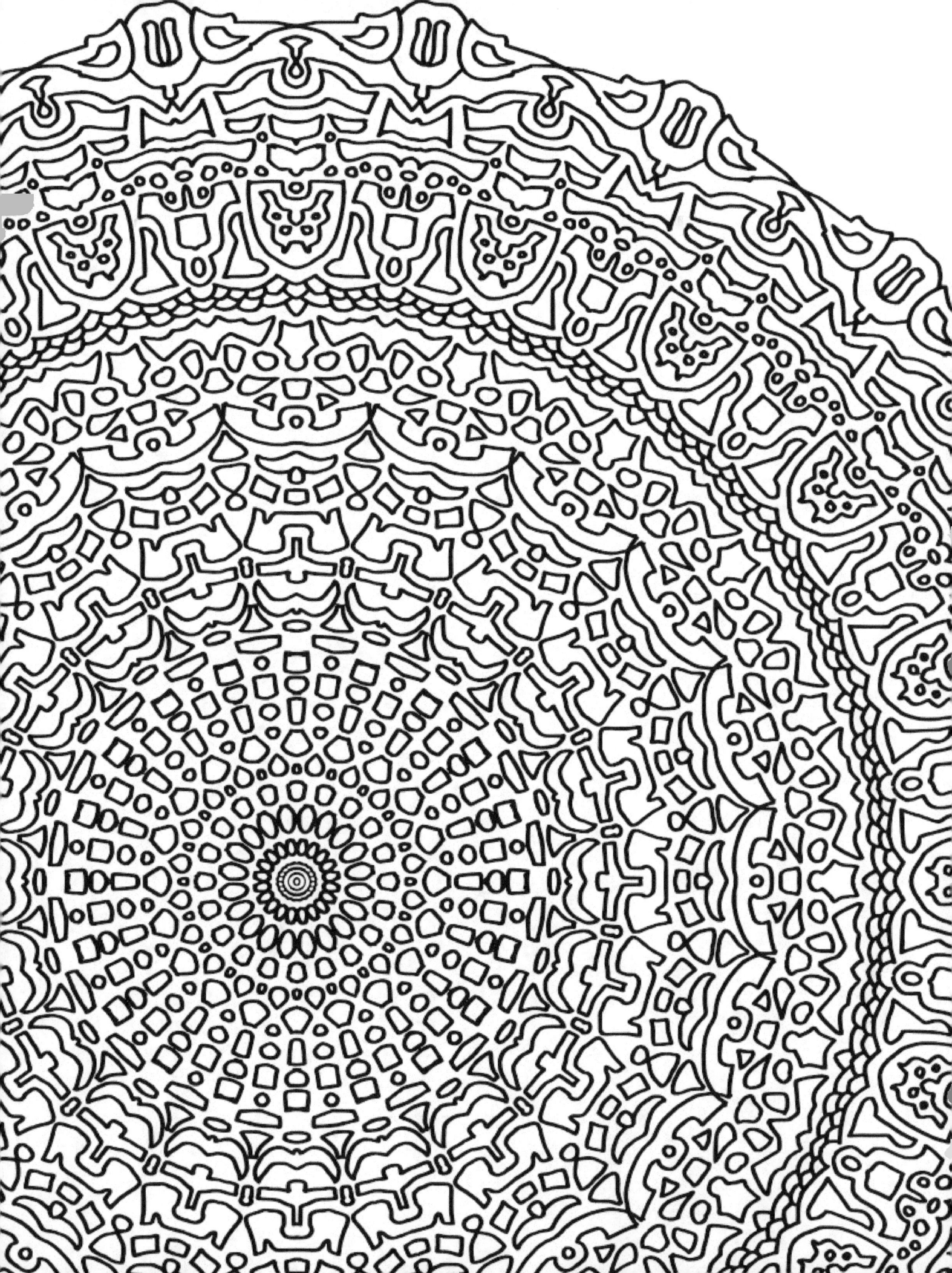

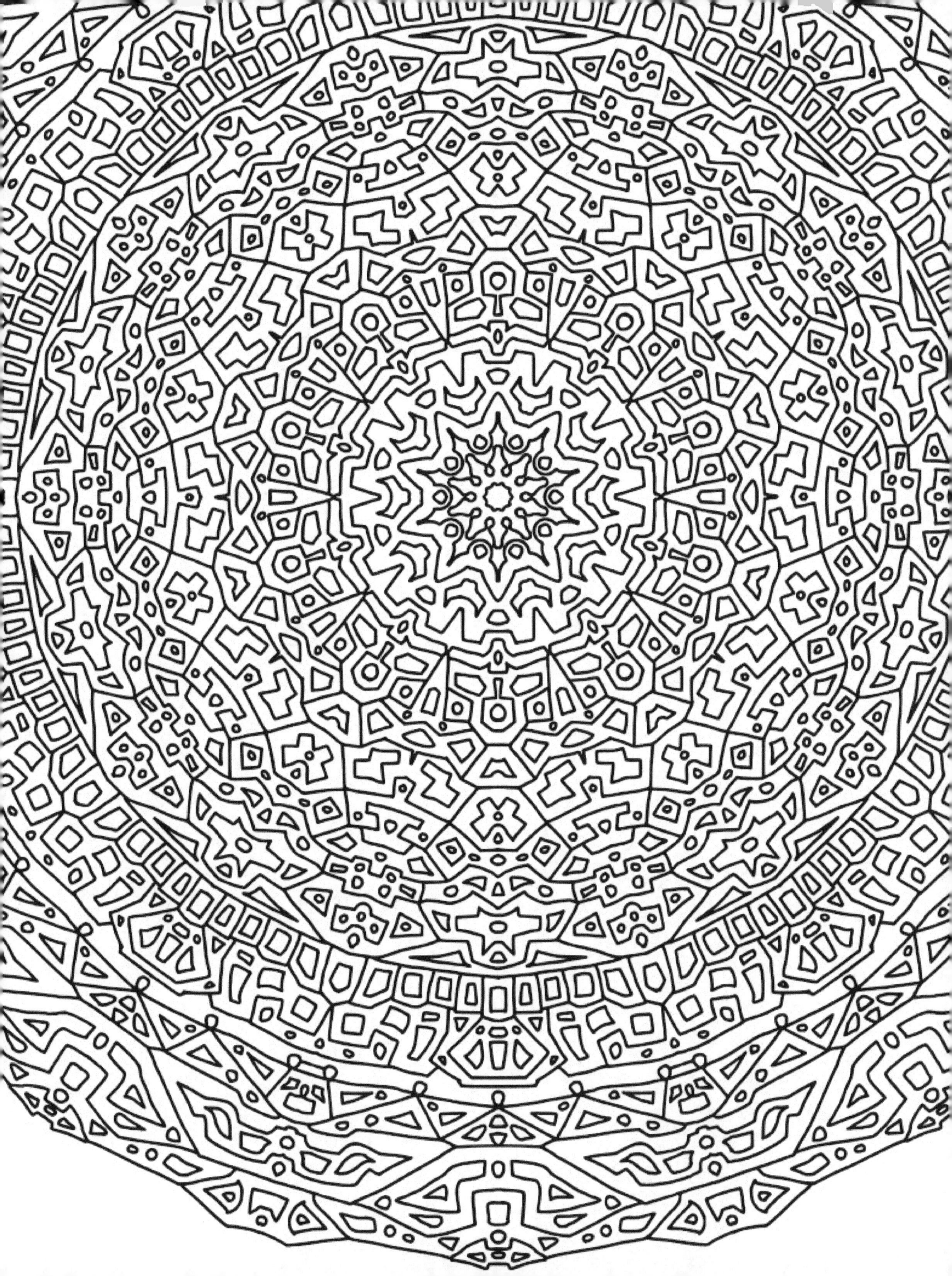

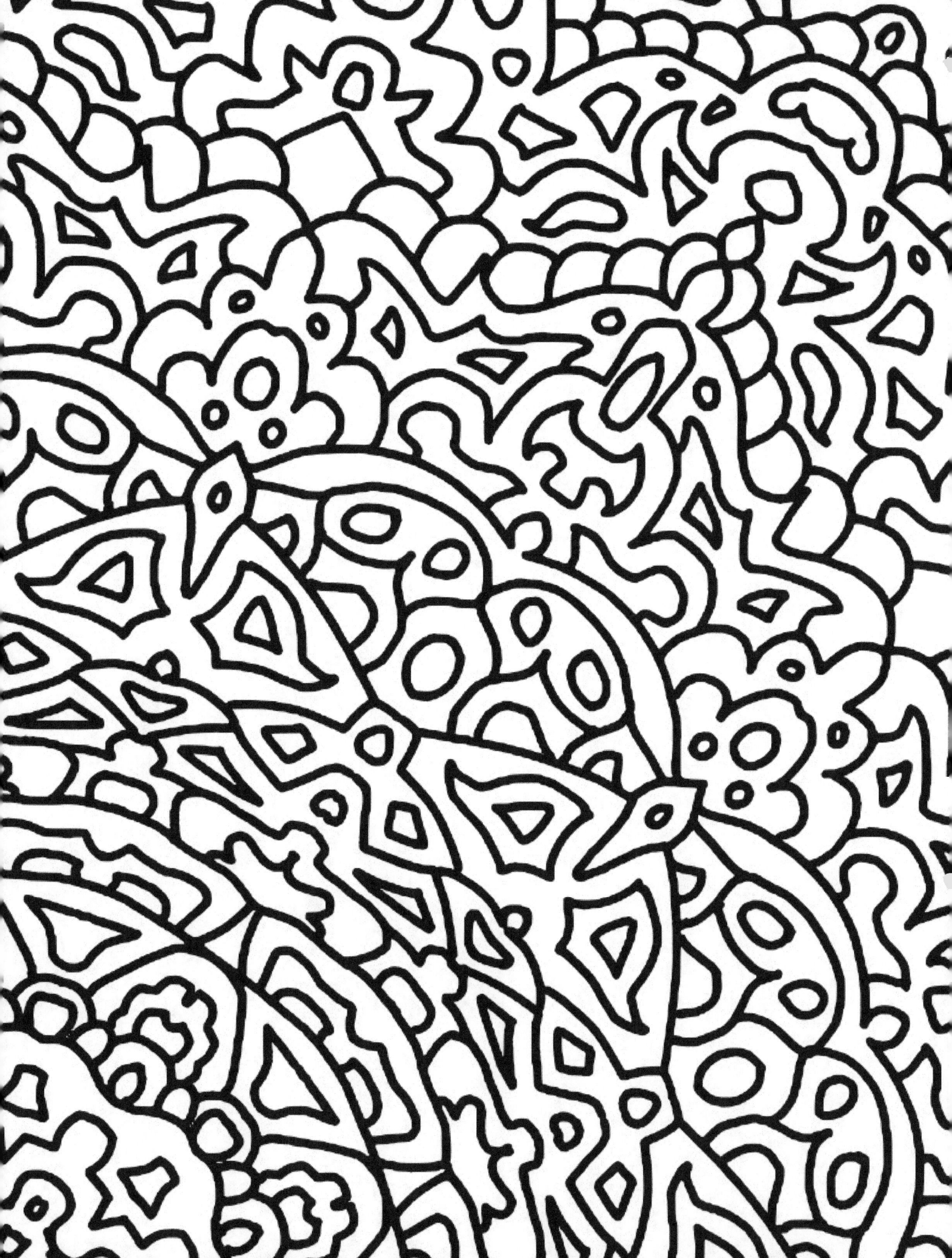

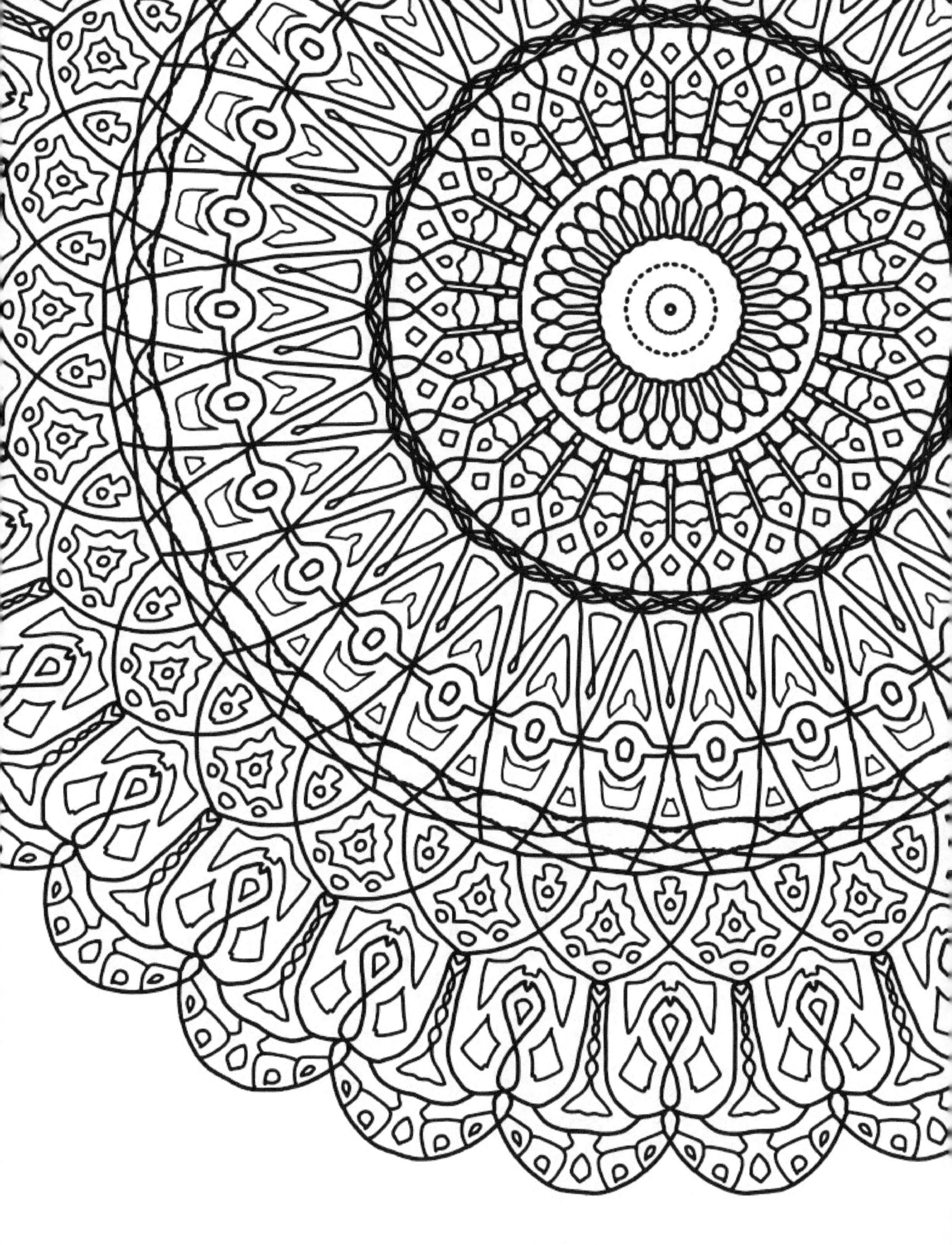

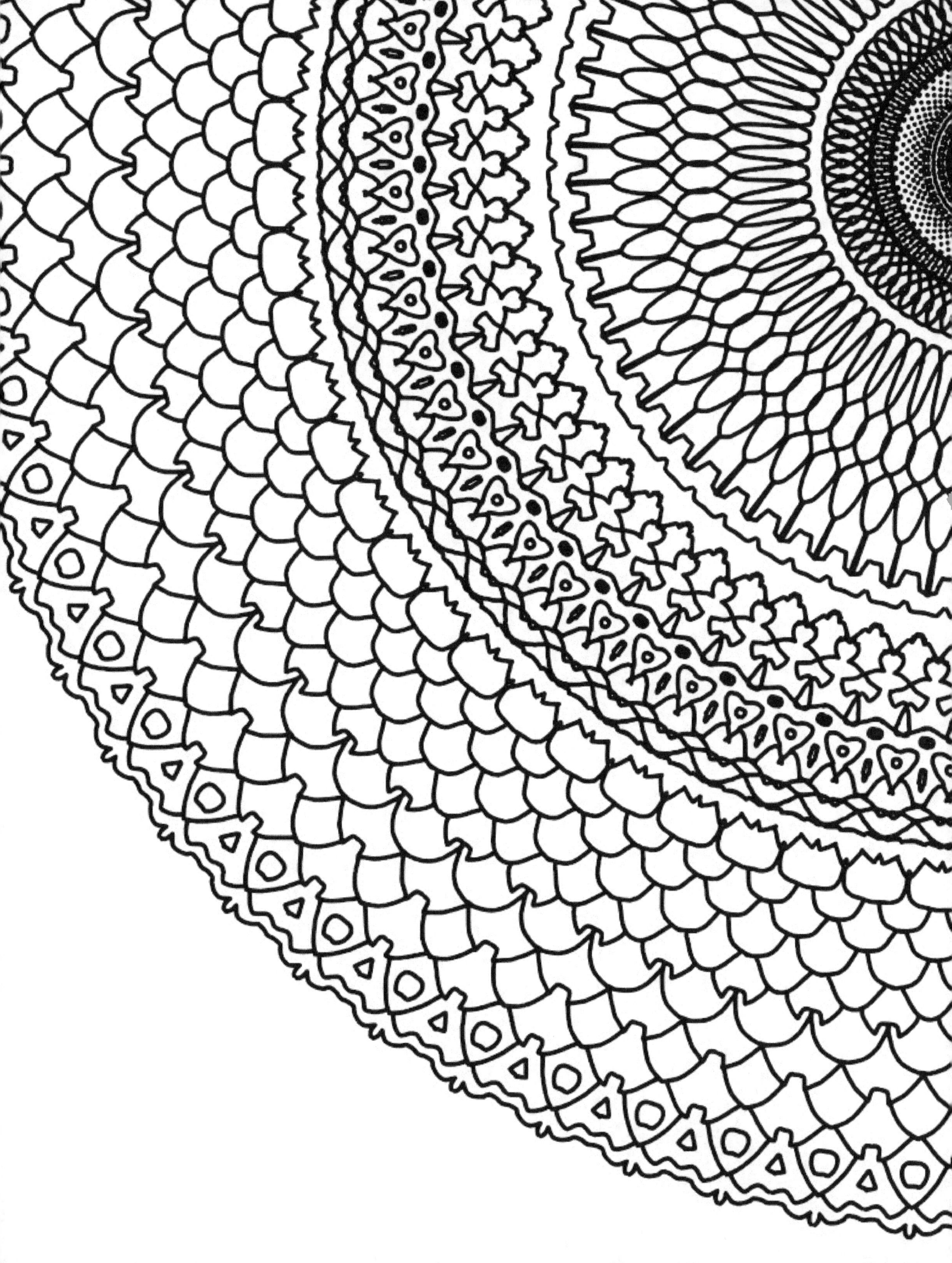

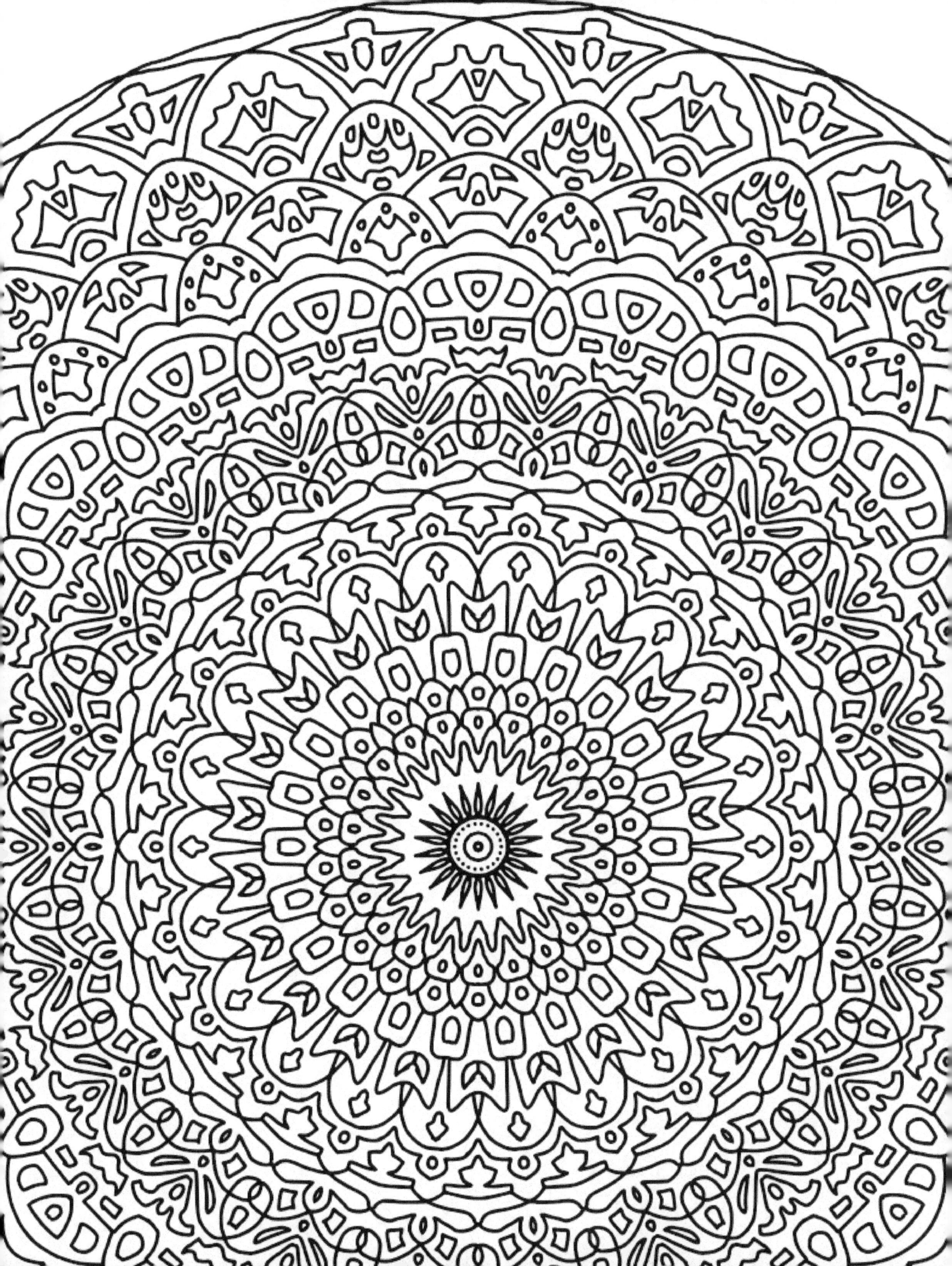

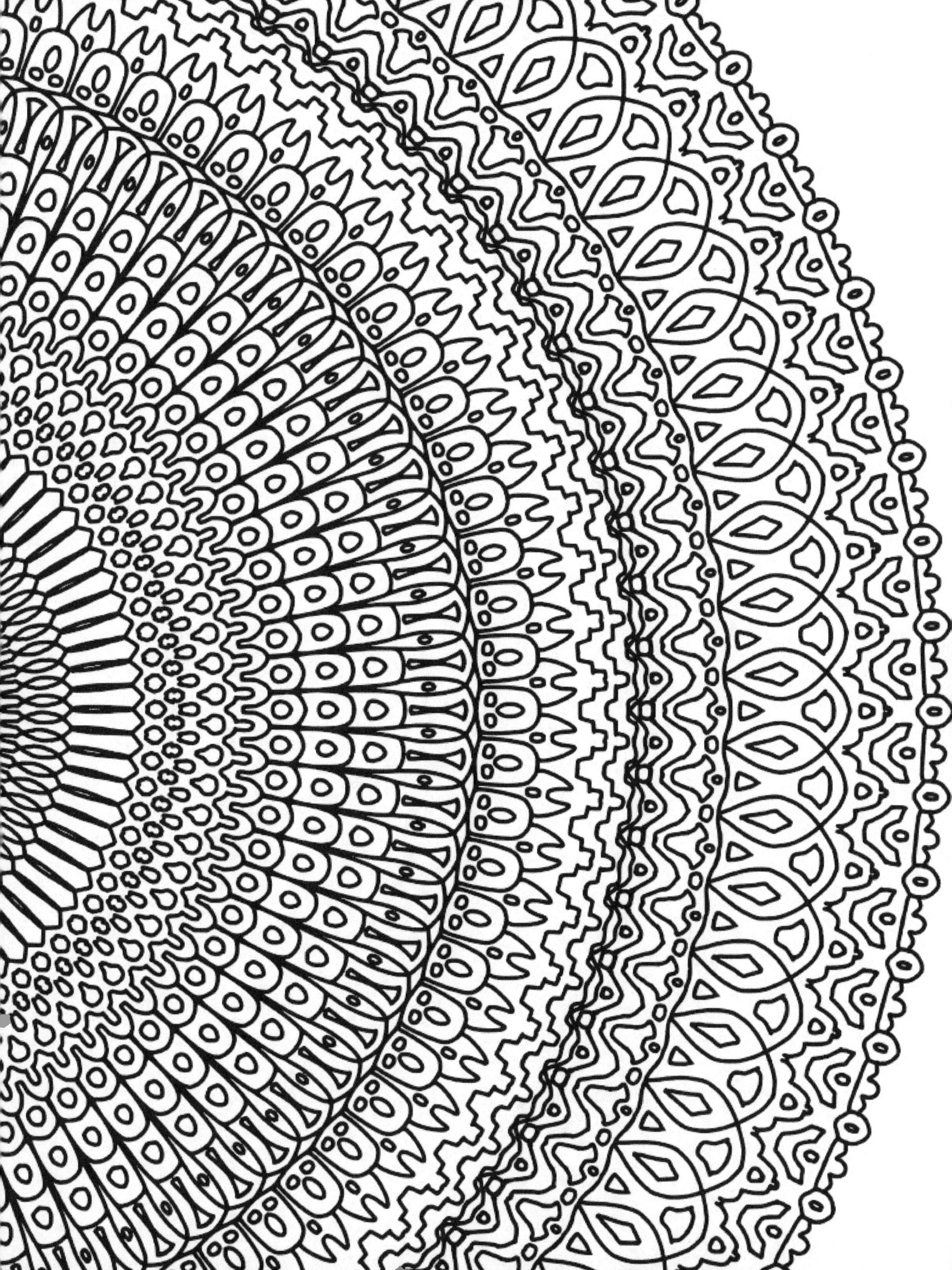

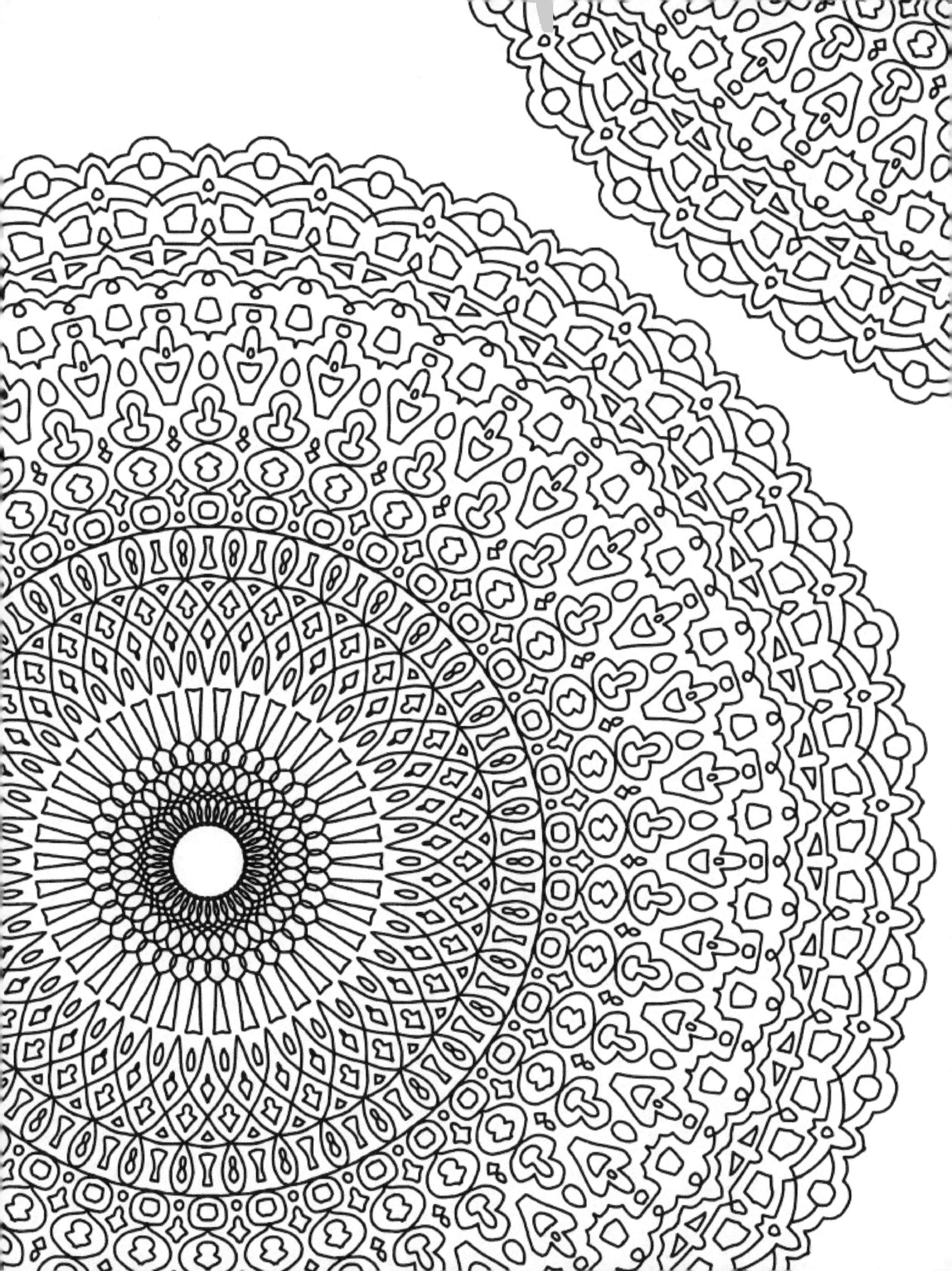

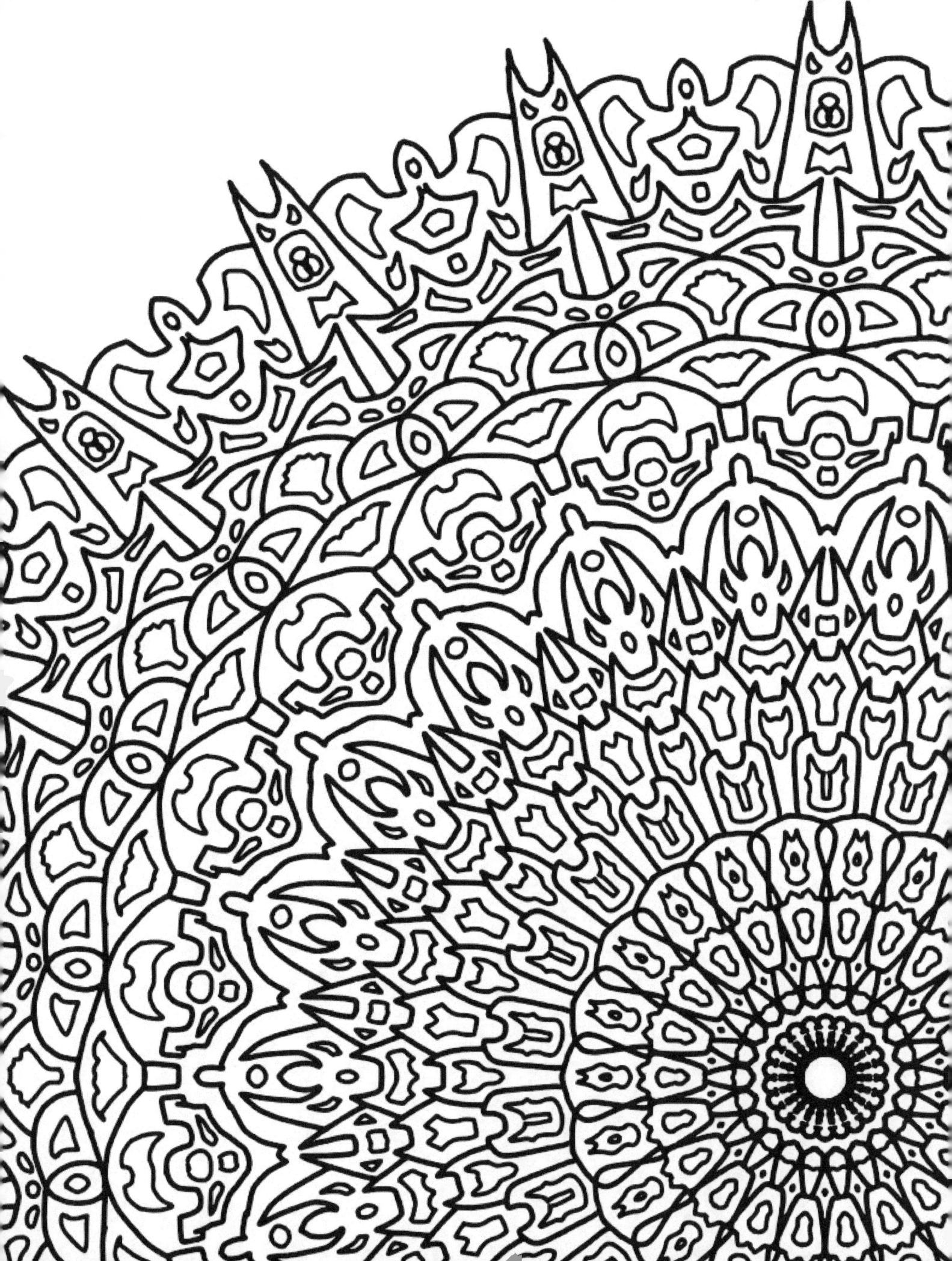

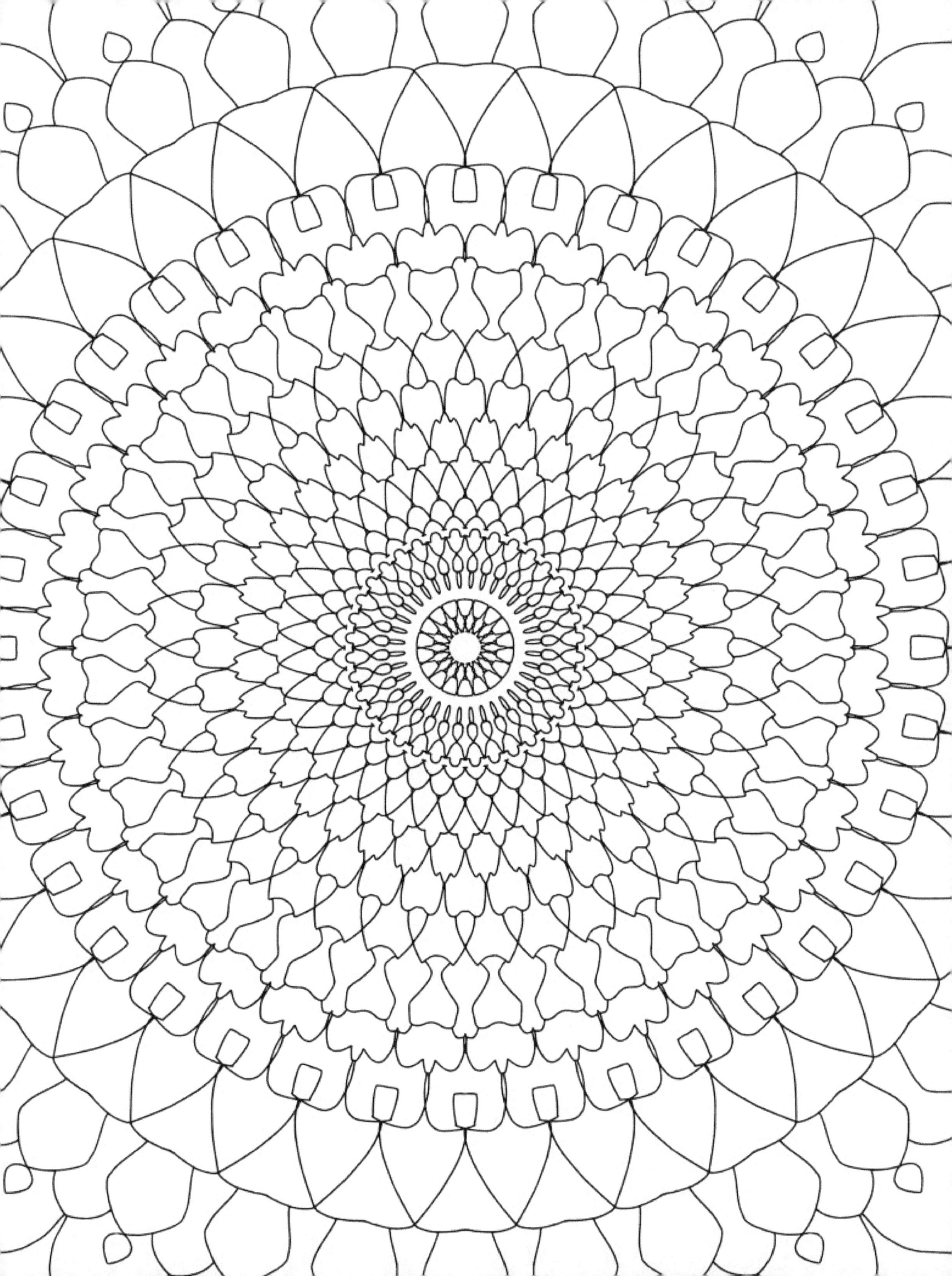

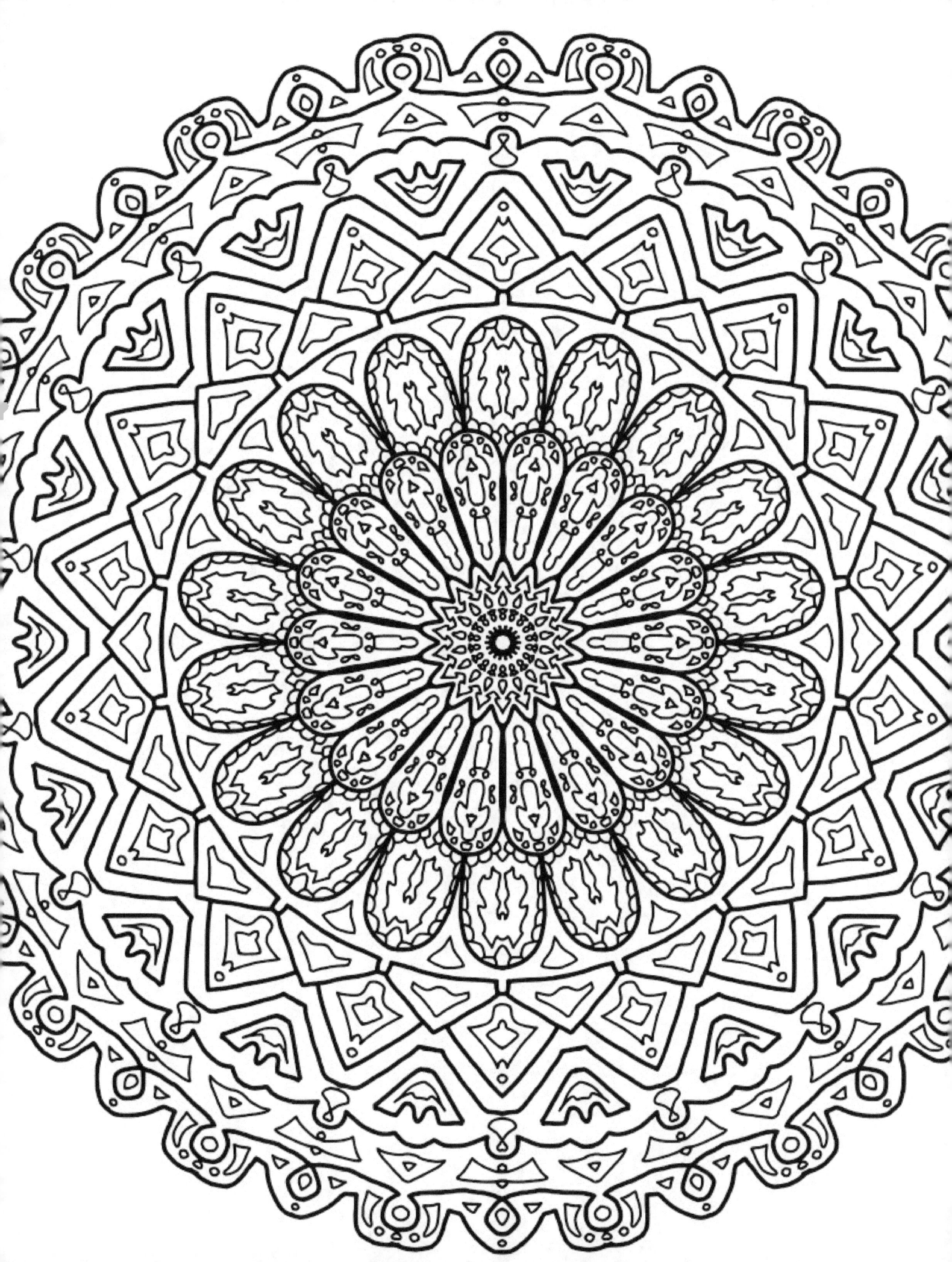

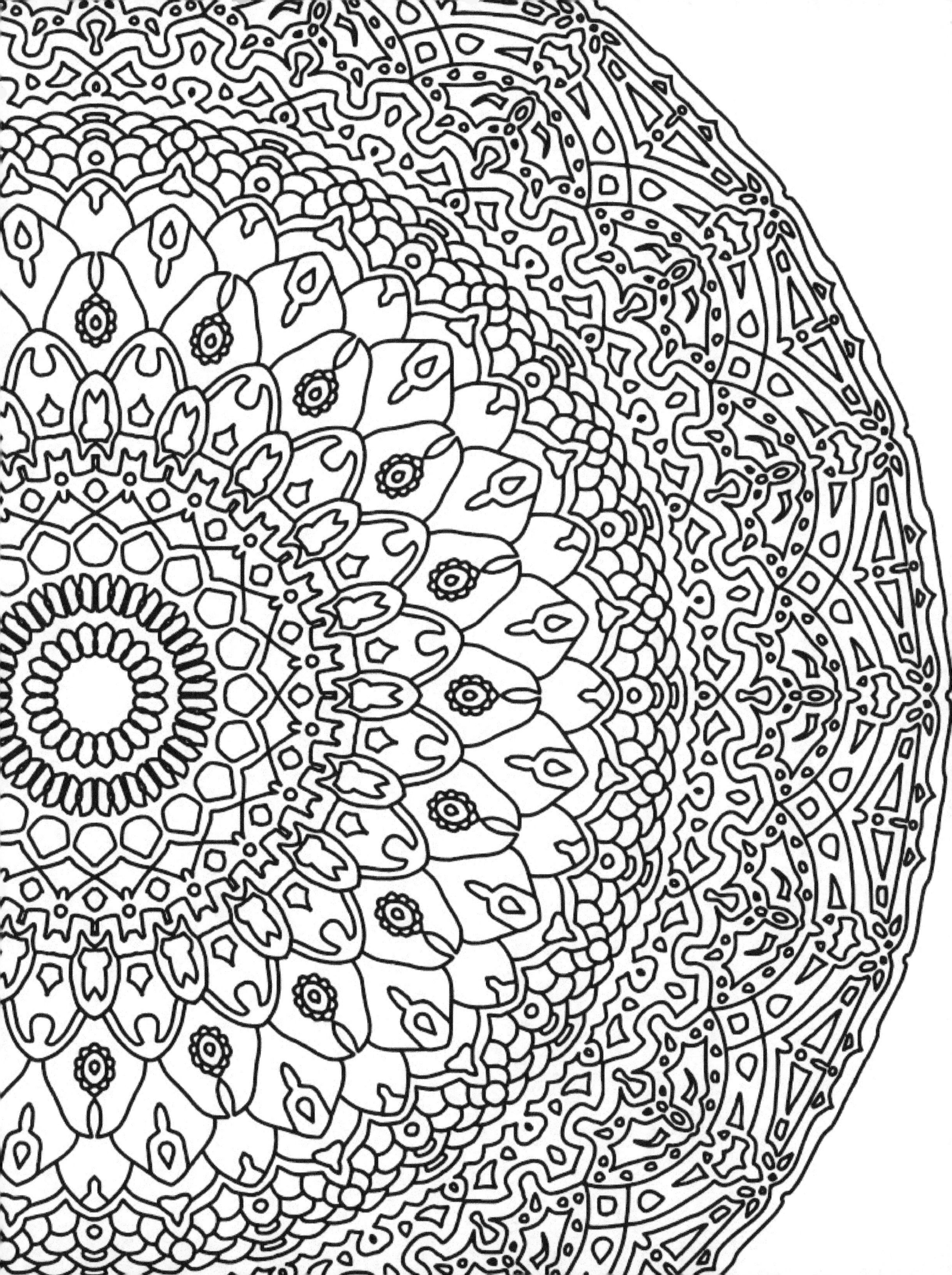

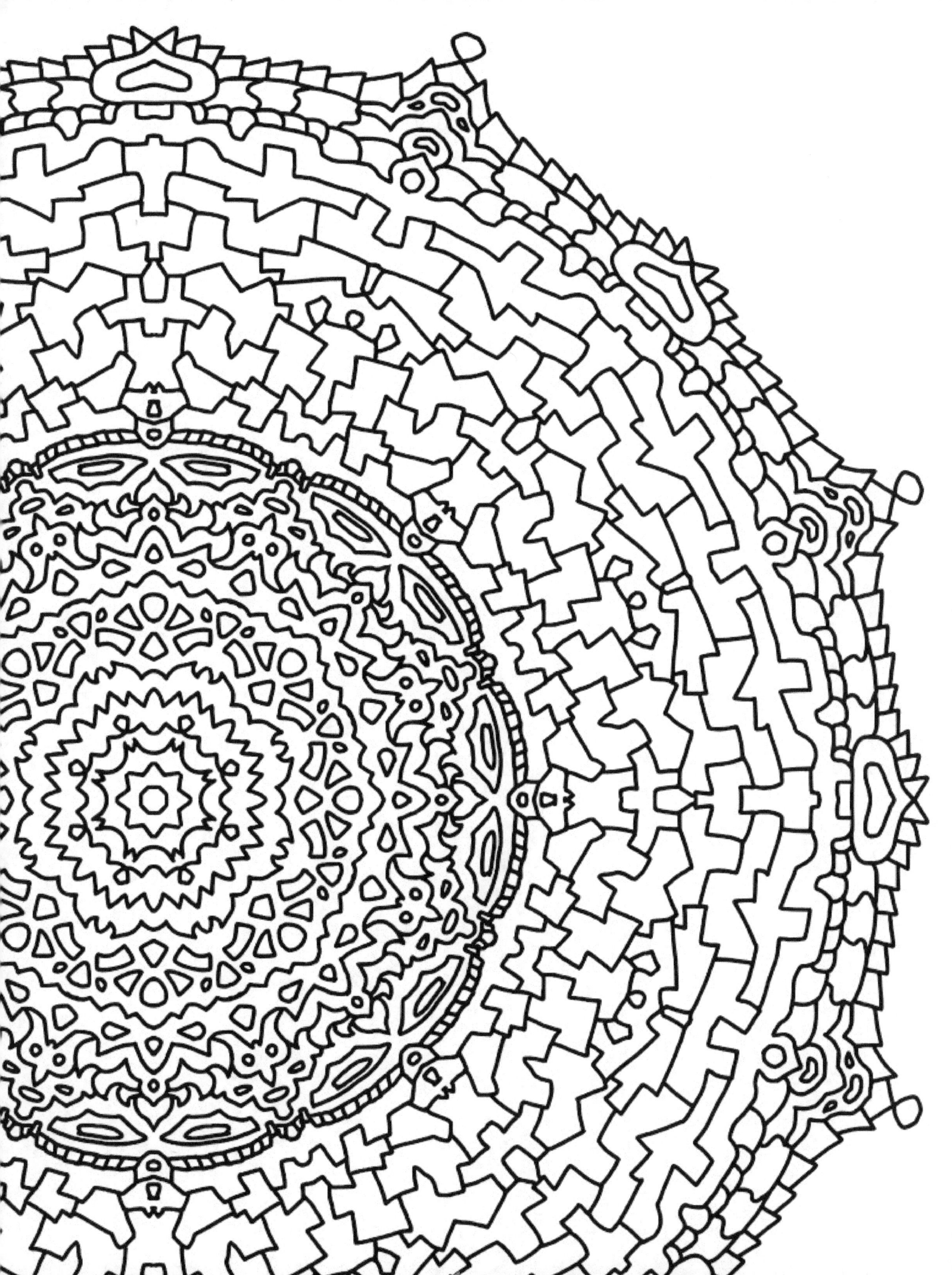

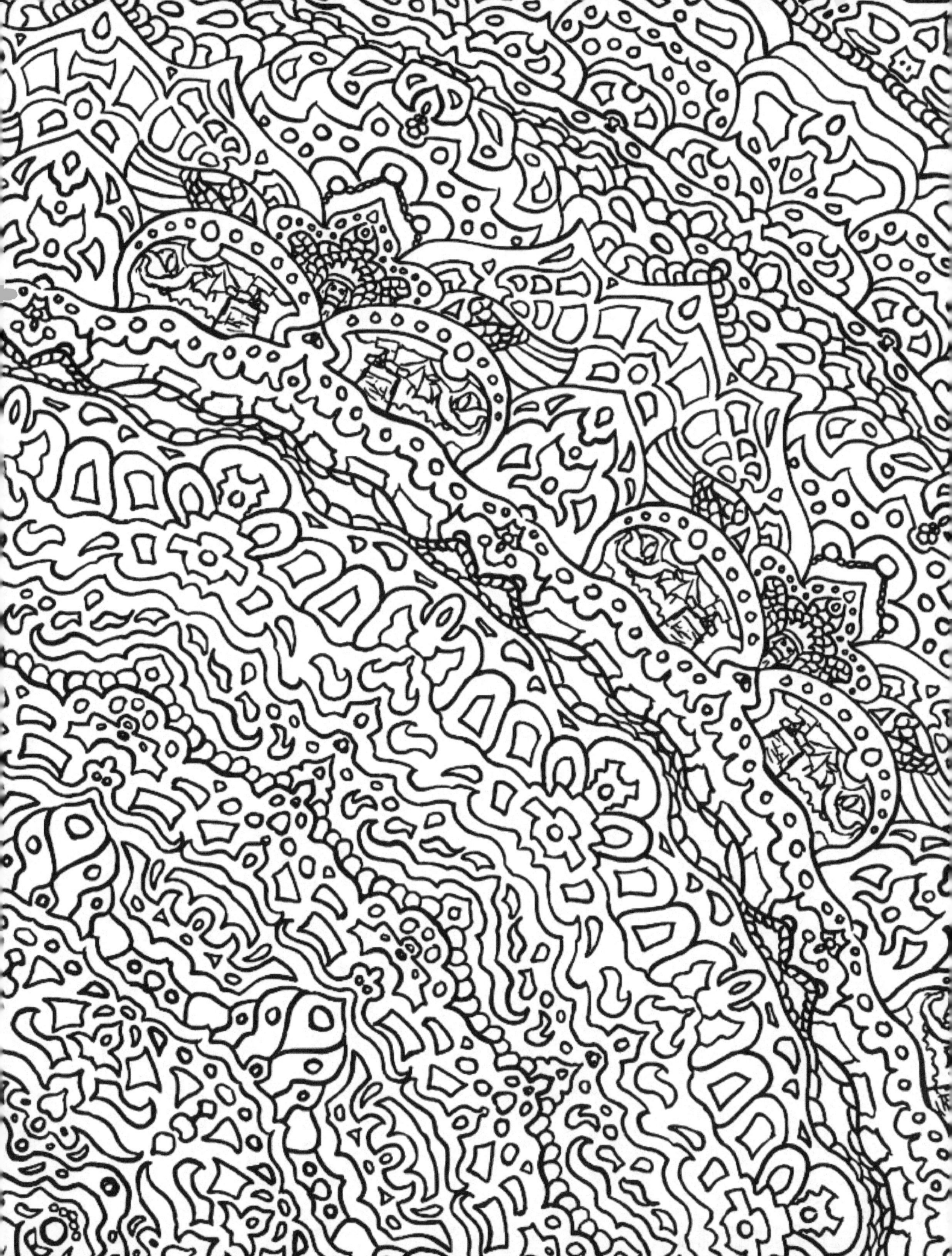

www.ingramcontent.com/pod-product-compliance
Lightning Source LLC
Chambersburg PA
CBHW080654190526
45169CB00006B/2118

* 9 7 8 1 5 3 3 1 0 0 9 7 9 *